La *nie*

Dec. '92

MARATHON

MARATHON

A STORY OF ENDURANCE AND FRIENDSHIP

RICHARD HARTEIS

W · W · NORTON & COMPANY

NEW YORK · LONDON

The text of this book is composed in 11/13 Avanta,
with display type set in Poster Bodoni Italic.
Composition and manufacturing by the Haddon Craftsmen, Inc.
Book design and title page art by Margaret M. Wagner.

First Edition

Library of Congress Cataloging in Publication Data
Harteis, Richard.
Marathon / by Richard Harteis.—1st ed.
p.   cm.
1. Marathon running—Training.   2. Friendship.   3. Poetry.   I. Title.
GV1065.17.T73H37   1989
796.42—dc20   89-33102

ISBN 0-393-02765-1

W. W. Norton & Company, Inc.
500 Fifth Avenue, New York, N. Y. 10110
W. W. Norton & Company Ltd.
37 Great Russell Street, London WC1B 3NU

1   2   3   4   5   6   7   8   9   0

FOR BETTY LUSSIER
MARATHON FRIEND

CONTENTS

EARL OF KENT: But who is with him?
A GENTLEMAN: None but the fool, who labors to outjest
His heart-struck injuries.

King Lear, III, i

PART ONE

—

RESOLVE

—

Two days ago I turned forty-one. It wasn't the momentous day that becoming forty or thirty or twenty-one was, but it had its own particular sting. An old Russian who is often part of my birthday celebrations told me over his vodka that now I was to begin to subtract the years. Not exactly a cheery sort of countdown when you think of it. Still, there was lobster and a rum cake and more champagne than anyone could drink. The conversation was bright, and as I served coffee in the kitchen it sounded as if twice as many guests as I'd invited had arrived.

Most of these guests were over sixty-five. When we're at our country house in Connecticut many of the friends we see are retired from the college where William taught before his stroke. We all drink too much and get into complicated disagreements, but on the whole these "oldbodies" are about as entertaining a group as you can find. They say one way to stay young is to hang out with people older than yourself. But lately my defense strategies against the middle-aged blues are wearing a little thin.

Earlier this summer I went to a small reunion for our college junior year abroad, and that buoyed me up some, surprisingly. It was touching to see what good people these friends had become. They were a bit arriviste, possibly, their politics become pragmatic with age, but there they all were, dancing to the Rolling Stones just like the old days, passing around photos of their teenage children, and catching up on one another's lives like a scene out of *The Big Chill.* Old animosities had disappeared, people paid attention when they spoke to one another, and they moved to the bar at brunch on Sunday with a certain earned weariness. Some of the women were more beautiful than they'd ever been, though crinkles around the eyes were universal. I imagine the gray hair on many of the men could no longer be called premature. I was glad not to be among their number, even if I imitated some of them with a slight paunch.

My nervousness about this reunion, however, was all wasted

energy. I was between jobs, fair enough, but I had just published a new book after seven years of silence. I hadn't become a millionaire, but I had done some good work in my life, a respectable if somewhat checkered career. It had been seventeen years since I'd met the friend with whom I was still sharing my life, and my classmates were sincerely happy for me.

An old flame, divorced, pretty as ever, wanted to know if I had "kept the faith." She remembered a line I had written for a hymn we sang at a secret folk mass in the Swiss mountains. As we passed around bread from the local bakery and glasses of jug wine that our chaplain had agreed to consecrate, we sang, "Christ hung burning from a golden tree, come down Jesus, come save me." What had I meant? How was I coping with the Church's homophobia? Did I know that two of our classmates had committed suicide? She showed me a picture of her little girl, who had the same sweet, crooked smile.

It didn't seem, twenty years later, that I had turned out so badly. Jack-of-all-trades, master maybe of none, but all my scars were well earned. I wasn't first in my class, but I wasn't last either. I guess I was swimming roughly in the middle of the school.

I wouldn't say I'm exactly satisfied with my life, though. No one ever is, I suppose. But the past few months have become something of a do-or-die situation for changing my life. Four years ago my dear William had a stroke, and I've been the caregiver ever since then while working pretty much full time at various professional positions. I've come to see what it's like to run a house and an office, cook meals, shop, pay bills, battle with Medicare, keep up William's correspondence, and try to maintain a lifetime of friendships that go back before the war. I guess there are plenty of working mothers who routinely manage this kind of life, but after four years I am getting a little frayed at the edges. And, unlike the children working mothers might care for, my charge will probably never grow to independence. Success for us is holding the line.

Since the stroke left William unable to speak much or read or write, I felt isolated. In addition I felt a profound loneliness, missing my old friend whose wit had always entertained, whose intelligence had always illuminated our life. And I was living with the daily sadness of watching this great American writer cope with being a prisoner in his own body. It became easier to schedule our activities in my own mind than to try to make him understand what the day held in store. On long drives to visit friends or going to his therapy classes, I would clam up. I began to eat and drink too much, became moody, short with sales clerks, impatient with William, surly. A prisoner of my rumination.

"How is Charlie Smith?" someone asked of a friend once at a dinner party. "Oh, he's fine," came the response. "He falls down and cries a lot, but otherwise he's fine."

A number of years ago I went back to school and became a physician's assistant. It has helped me save William's life on a number of occasions, I suppose, but it has also helped me see that I was in trouble from time to time. The manuals warn about the danger of wallowing in one's role as victim. Alcoholism and depression can sneak up on you, and the next thing you know the caregiver is in need of care.

William and I have been a lot luckier than many, though. Things are tough at times, but our life together is filled with light, our love deepens, and the "glamour" of sharing William's life hasn't diminished. His stepmother (in her mid-nineties and very sharp) set up a trust fund after the stroke that enables us to keep a winter house in the D.C. suburbs and maintain the Connecticut farm for use in the summer. There are various cars and boats and other toys to play with, and if we want to visit friends in Europe or sponsor a reception for a friend's exhibition, we can just do it. William always took care not to be pushed around by money, a quality in his character I've tried to imitate. I don't *think* I let money influence my goals or decisions in life unduly, or enter into how I value people. Certainly, money doesn't compensate for poor health, but I can understand a lot better now the tragedy of the elderly poor in this country. It doesn't seem fair to work hard your whole life sacrificing for others and then live final anxious, crimped years for the lack of money. I don't plan to let it happen to me. The caregivers who do it somehow without adequate resources are the real heroes.

William is the only American to win the Vaptsarov Prize, something like the Eastern Bloc's Nobel Prize, and so we travel to that part of the world as guests of the state from time to time. Other awards and special recognitions brighten his career these days, but perhaps the luckiest charm in our life remains our friends.

Over the years Betty has been one of the most loyal of these friends, something like a bodyguard, spiritual adviser, and financial counselor combined. She and I met jogging on the streets of Rabat in 1980, where she had come as a consultant to develop economic opportunities for women and I was serving as health officer on a project to build a new radar system for the Moroccan air force. It was something like a golden period in my life. Policemen saluted me after they checked my papers if I got stopped for speeding. I had a town house and a beach house, and I even had a helicopter at my disposal if I needed to get somewhere fast in an emergency. William visited me five times during my work there and got to be Betty's good friend too.

After raising four sons and too many years pretending to enjoy the role of Mediterranean society queen, Betty went back to graduate school and set up a consulting firm in the United States. Her years as a pilot and counterintelligence operative in World War II tested her mettle and left her uncompromising about what sort of foolishness she would tolerate in life. She isn't pushy about her advice, but like a teacher or politician, she isn't reluctant to give it either. More than her vast experience, though, or even her good will and unpretentious common sense, the most valuable thing about her is her absolute honesty. She never hedges her bets by saying, "Of course, it's your life and ultimately you'll have to decide." More likely it's "Now you've got to quit your job and enjoy your life with William for the summer," or "Why don't you run with me in the New York City Marathon this year and get rid of that gut? It will be good for you. You're getting a little strung out lately."

So here I am, two hundred pounds plus, still carrying too much weight to train comfortably, but making it. At six weeks into my training, though, and with ten weeks left until the race, I'm still not on target in my training. I should be up to thirty-seven miles a week, and I've only done twenty-five. I'm a little thinner, and now the four-mile run to Fort Shantok along the Thames River is not a real hardship. I'm hardly out of breath at all by the time I get to the site where Uncas is said to have buried his princess. If I can start getting up earlier, it will be cooler, and I'll have my run out of the way before it's time to begin William's day. And, if I can limit my drinking to two martinis a day, my friend Charlie says getting up early will be no problem. I guess I'll get serious about this New York Marathon. Betty runs it each year, and as she says, "You can walk twenty-six miles, can't you?" A few weeks ago a sprained ankle kept me from running, and I suppose a more serious injury could ruin my plans. Or a Mack truck could come around the bend and do me in. It would be a pity to go through all this for nothing.

A little earlier this summer we visited friends in the country who have forsaken city life and taken to raising horses year-round in the hills of New Hampshire. Wonderful people, but so self-congratulatory about how hard they worked, how healthy they were, how beautiful their garden was, how svelte their coronary arteries, how superb their homemade jam. They made you feel like a moral degenerate if you weren't out of bed by 8:00 A.M. And perhaps keeping a record of my progress will seem just as self-congratulatory—if I make it, that is. But if one heavy-drinking, mildly overweight, middle-aged, overburdened, B-minus poet can change his spots a little by using the structure of a marathon run, perhaps it will be a useful account.

William says of an imaginary painter in one of his poems,

> Man and artist, he is working on his ways
> so that when he becomes set in them
> as old people must, for all that their souls
> clap hands, for all that their spirits dance,
> his ways will have grace, his pictures will have class.

And surely this was William's own intention before his illness. I used to watch him almost physically restrain himself from delivering a well-deserved reproach, or extend a generous opinion by sheer force of will. It's the only way I can imagine he survived the insult of the stroke. Often stroke patients plunge into depression, and their lexicon turns dark and foul in the face of their tragedy. But his sort of manners and dignity and courage are qualities that don't just happen. They are as hard earned as the seemingly effortless elegance in his verse.

In classic culture the highest manifestation of love between friends was the ability to inspire the desire for the good in each other. Robert Frost told William once that he'd have respected him if for nothing more than the thirty-two night landings on a carrier deck William had made in the Pacific as a navy pilot. In these past years I've seen even greater examples of guts.

I expect there will be some dark days in my future. Last summer I had a little cancer cut out of the bladder; it's the kind they say is not life threatening but often returns. We are none of us getting any younger. Many of the people I love are considerably older than I. And there are the dear parents and siblings whom I have come to love so too. My baby sister Judy will be forty in six days. It seems incredible. I try to maintain a faith that we will all get out alive, but in the process a lot is required of us. And if William is right, fortunate responses to life are more than genetic. We have to *train*, it seems, especially when our life gets a little fat, our soul a little out of shape.

August 20. Day one.

PART TWO

TRAINING

Monday is an off day, according to the training schedule the New York Road Runners Club sends the first-time marathoner. All sixteen weeks are laid out for you like an insurance agent's chart listing the various options at any given age for purchasing coverage.

Today is the first day of week seven on the schedule. I'm already late in my training if I hope to run the New York City Marathon. "You'll be late for your own funeral," my dad is fond of saying to me—which I wouldn't mind so much. He also likes to remind me that it's all downhill for me now that I'm past forty. I'm beginning to wonder why I didn't just take a couple of aspirin the morning after my birthday party and go back to bed like most folks who are tempted to make mid-life resolutions. I have vowed to be one of twenty-two thousand runners who will

THE FIRST-TIME MARATHON FOUR-MONTH TRAINING SCHEDULE
(from a 25-mile-a-week base)

WEEK	MON.	TUES.	WED.	THURS.	FRI.	SAT.	SUN.	TOTAL MILEAGE
1	Off	4	4	4	4	3	6	25
2	Off	4	5	4	4	3	8	28
3	Off	4	5	4	5	2	10	30
4	Off	4	6	4	5	4	10	33
5	Off	4	6	5	6	4	12	37
6	Off	4	6	4	5	4	14	37
7	Off	4	6	4	6	4	16	40
8	Off	6	6	4	6	6	12	40
9	Off	4	6	4	4	4	18	40
10	Off	6	6	4	6	6	14	42
11	Off	4	6	4	6	5	20	45
12	Off	6	6	5	8	6	14	45
13	Off	5	6	4	6	6	18	45
14	Off	4	6	6	6	4	14	40
15	Off	6	6	5	4	10	4	35
16 Race Week	Off	4	6	4	Off	2	RaceDay Marathon	16+ Race

Aug. 24 → (at week 6)
Nov. 1 → (at week 16 Race Week)

NOTE: When you race you may need to adjust your daily and weekly mileage downward. Do not attempt to combine long runs and races on the same day or weekend.

Reproduced by permission from *The Runner's Handbook*, copyright 1985 by Bob Glover and Jack Shepherd.

gather in New York City on November 1 in an attempt to try to run 26.2 miles. What have I done?

In the D.C. Marathon the marines put up a huge sign at the twenty-mile mark with painted-on cartoon characters scrambling to get over the top of "the Wall" any way they can. The Wall is the mystical point in the marathon when the body gives out, when there are no reserves left, and every runner who makes it to that point must come up with some spiritual force to counter the immovable object in front of him. I feel like a new recruit who is about to meet his drill sergeant on the first day of boot camp.

Yesterday I patted myself on the back all day because I ran around the "block" twice. Our block is actually a 3.2-mile oval along the river cutting through thick green woods in rural Connecticut. Our neighbors are working-class families who build submarines over at Electric Boat or take care of the college. They have done pretty well for themselves, though, and the homes are maintained with much pride and love of privacy. It's a pretty run and long enough to keep you interested with different sights as you go.

Unfortunately, my "big" run was just ten miles short of the run I should have made at that point in my training schedule. Betty tends to be a little cavalier about these schedules, thinks you can get started later than they say and still finish in the pack on race day. It might be well into September before she tries a really long run out on Staten Island where she lives. Of course, Betty has run the marathon any number of times and can afford to be a little more cavalier. I wish she lived closer so we could train together. First time out, I suspect I should try to play by the rules. I've got ten weeks to try to get a little closer to the forty–fifty miles a week I'm supposed to be running.

Even so, my measly little 6.5 miles yesterday was pretty exhilarating. I managed to run every day last week in spite of the heat, houseguests, and minor strains, and I felt the runs getting easier every day just the way they're supposed to. I couldn't wait to lace up my shoes in the morning and get that extra bounce you feel as the muscles warm up.

The leaves haven't begun to change yet. The quiet country roads are still green woodland tunnels lined by stone walls that the colonial farmers erected as they cleared the fields of granite rocks. But the first brisk air of autumn arrived yesterday, and as the road straightened out along the high bank on the river it was as if someone had just washed the windows clean after a long gray winter. Good sleeping weather, but not for me so much these days if I am to succeed.

The Thames River at our shore is a mile wide. Deep green marsh grass spreads like a carpet down to the shining black water. The tide pulls brackish water in and out even this far up from New London, and the channel is deep. The swans have become numerous enough almost to be a nuisance. Last summer I fell asleep reading on the Point, and one large bird woke me with a start. He was like a 747 taking off from the runway just three feet over my head. He was as scared as I was as I jumped up into his flight path.

There are too few neighbors to cause much traffic on the Thames, and sometimes when we take the dory out for a sail we have the river all to ourselves. The first year we launched the *Svetlana* even my dreams had the little wooden shell cut the waves with an exciting beauty that was almost sexual. A coal miner's son from Pennsylvania with erotic dreams about sailing his Swampscot dory. Astonishing.

The Greeks believed that a place this beautiful is inhabited by minor gods, or at least has a sort of resident spirit. Mikey, our yellow Lab, is certainly happier here than in the city and on occasion goes a little wacky even when we haven't seen a stranger on the road or a fox popping out of nowhere. There's a dappled corner in the woods across from our road marked off by rotting split-rail fences. Five diminutive tombstones dating back to 1824 go on lamenting children of the Smith family, who used to farm this land. I always say a little prayer for their souls as I come by that corner, offer up my own pain for any they might still be going through and ask them to help me in my own affairs if they're in a position to put in a good word for me. Most of the fields have gone back to second growth, and there are different

generations here now, "second growth, and second growth," as
William says. Still, they are part of this land.

When I ran around the block for the first time yesterday, I
hadn't gone far enough certainly for any sort of endorphin high,
but the tightness in my pelvis had washed away with a few
minutes of particularly long strides. The sky was a deep Arizona
blue in that thin air, so clean and refreshing I wasn't a bit
winded. And the flimsy nylon shorts I was wearing felt like nothing at all, like running naked. When I reached the driveway and
was about to turn in for the finish, it just seemed natural to keep
going.

Last month when my friend Philip came up for the weekend
from New York we ran around the block together. The first time
around he was barely out of breath, still prancing his high butt
and teasing me about being out of shape. He had to run around
the block a second time on his own. Last month I wasn't up to it.

It had been twenty years since I'd last seen Philip, but he
looked younger than the day we said goodbye in Switzerland.
When we caught up with each other at the class reunion earlier
this summer, I couldn't believe all the stories I'd heard about
him after his divorce. The scuttlebutt had Philip throwing his
life away, drinking himself to death, crashing cars, hustling a
meager life as a ski bum in Aspen. But the Philip I met at the
reunion had put all that behind.

My houseguest was so sensationally good-looking, so put together, the neighborhood wives made pitifully transparent excuses just to come over and meet him. Philip had given up drinking, managed it somehow on his own without Alcoholics
Anonymous or Antabuse, and worked his way up to be vice
president in a large international shipping firm. He traveled to
Rio or Tokyo as though he were going to dinner with a friend
across town. Multilingual, self-assured, fairly rich, and wearing
designer clothes, old Philip had become a caricature from some
Harlequin romance. Like Alexander the Great, he doesn't even
seem to have an odor when he sweats. I lent him the skimpiest
bathing suit I could find and tried not to be too obvious taking in
his sculptured torso throughout the weekend.

Philip's father had died from a stroke, and unlike other guests, he paid careful attention to William during the visit without patronizing him. His sensitivity was very moving. He was intuitive about what I was going through too as the caregiver. "We all have to decide how far our love will go when tragedy strikes, Rich," he said. "Whether it's a parent or a lover or a wife. We all get our chance."

I think he'd be proud of me that I went around the block a second time. I'd like to please him the way you would try to impress an older brother. It isn't going to be easy running this course six days a week for ten more weeks, and I've got to motivate myself however I can. Is it in *Death in Venice* where Mann describes two kinds of genius, the inspired, flash-in-the-pan sort and the kind built on day-in, day-out, sticking-at-it-no-matter-what until all the little pieces build into a formidable achievement? That's the kind of thinking I'll need to run this marathon. Day by day till I become strong. Little by little going beyond my limits. Keeping at it throughout the years until you outlive your critics, that's the genius of the artist. But the discipline is not easily won.

At one point along the road Philip and I stopped to inspect a tree filled with brilliant purple blossoms glowing in the morning sunshine. We picked a few, smelled them, rubbed the petals between our fingers.

"I think it's rose of Sharon, Philip."

"Naw, it's oleander. It used to grow around our garden in Cairo," he said.

"Better be careful, it's narcotic, I think. Don't little babies die in their sleep rocking under the oleander?"

Sometimes I stop along the road to pick a few wildflowers for the studio when we have guests coming. The purple tree has come to magnificent full bloom now. I wish Philip were here to see it each morning. I always take a blossom and tuck it in the key pocket of my shorts when I run by, or just brush the flowers with my fingertips.

Monitoring your body while training for a marathon is a little like teaching yourself how to write. You have to pay attention to what is being played out, listen to your instincts, make the subconscious conscious. And you have to keep at it even when it becomes painful, or the weather turns nasty, or your imagination has completely dried up. If you do keep at it, though, one day you'll run ten miles or come up with an image that you know is perfect, that will move a reader as much as it has surprised you.

Once you've conditioned yourself to the point where your breathing is still regular as the miles roll on and you can pretty much forget about early morning stiffness in the calves and thighs, you're faced with lots of free time to ruminate while the machine purrs down the road. The loneliness of the long-distance runner. This is why some people find running so boring, I suppose, like waiting in a dentist's office to have a cavity drilled out, or standing on line hungry at the grocery store.

Runners deal with this occupational hazard in a lot of different ways. Mostly they try to find a partner to help egg them on, or perhaps they join a running club. When Betty first got me running with her in Morocco, we spent the morning run gossiping about social life in Rabat or discussing our problems at work. It's amazing how intimate you can become plugging up some hill, half out of breath, not even looking your partner in the eye. In the beginning I couldn't run a mile, but I came to like the company so much, enjoyed the chance to find out who was really doing what in Rabat, that I began to push it to two or three.

Philip uses his time on long runs to meditate. I do too, I suppose, but not with the formal oriental discipline I suspect Philip uses. Susan Shreve dreams up plots while she's swimming long laps in the community pool, writes novels and takes care of an old back injury at the same time. Maxine Kumin told me once she writes her poems while she's mucking out the stalls for her horses. Running is a little like that for me, I guess. Often I run with a Walkman and let Rod Stewart or Mozart inspire me up those hills.

For a while I held the tape deck while I ran, and later in the day my fingers would begin to twitch uncontrollably like Dr. Strangelove's alien arm trying to strangle him. I was sure I was having little seizures from a brain tumor until I realized that my tight grasp on the radio was causing the problem. Sure enough, the twitching disappeared just as the knife pain between my shoulder blades did when I stopped running with my hands tightened into fists. Lately when I've run I've just been mucking around inside, like Maxine cleaning out her stables, trying to make a little sense of things once I've let the body slip into remote control.

I learned how to work out my problems while I was running last winter. The technique proved to be a real lifesaver those weeks I spent with William when he lay dying.

An old Peace Corps friend now with the State Department in Haiti had invited William and me down for a couple of weeks' sun this past February. His new wife was adapting to the Third World well enough, but they liked importing friends and treating them to the rich expatriate life when they got homesick.

Most people would hardly consider Haiti a tourist paradise, but I loved running the mountain roads in the morning and coming back for a swim before William got up to have his breakfast. Pretty hard not to be conspicuous as I ran, but the people teased me good-naturedly and I joked back in Creole. A couple of women would start jogging with the "blanc," and that got the whole street giggling, a white man being chased by a woman with bucket and broom.

The number of people Dick employed to look after his life was a little embarrassing given his mission with the embassy, but things were certainly very comfortable. Our host was, after all, providing a livelihood for people in a country with the highest unemployment rate in the hemisphere. Servants tended to the house, kept the grounds lush as an oasis. High walls camouflaged with red and purple bougainvillea surrounded the swimming pool and terrace. A servant stood in the shadows waiting for a mango to fall into the aquamarine water or for someone to call for a drink. Now and then we could hear voodoo drums in the hills, just the right exotic touch.

But on the night before our departure the serpent entered the garden and ruined this Paradise. As I finished packing, turned the light off and said good night, William informed me he had appendicitis. That didn't seem very likely to me, but he did seem to have some tenderness when I turned the light back on and palpated his belly.

When someone has had as many medical problems as William has had, you have to learn to be a little balanced in how you react to such a complaint. The medical history requires a high index of suspicion, but if you go to the emergency room every time there's a stomachache, you can turn the patient into a hypochondriac, driving yourself crazy in the process. Still, William's pain *was* just at McBurney's point, which is usually the case in appendicitis, and it seemed to be the characteristic rebound pain as well. But there was no fever, no rock-hard abdomen, no vomiting yet, or any real distress. Just to be sure, I talked it over with Dick and we called a considerate Haitian physician to make a house call.

In elderly patients appendicitis is a hard diagnosis to make, and the doctor was as unsure as I was about what to do. It might be anything from a kidney stone to cancer. He offered to hospitalize William for observation but said we might risk returning to our own country for care if William didn't feel much worse by the time our flight took off early next morning.

Dick was extremely kind and full of good wishes as he drove us to the airport at dawn, but it was a sad and very uncertain farewell. William kept his eyes closed sitting in the wheelchair and didn't speak at all. He didn't thrash around or call out on the plane, but his face deepened its grimace during the long flight. I hadn't slept since his pain began, and every time he sighed or gave a little moan I'd feel my heart kick up with a surge of adrenalin. When we reached Miami he was clammy and gray. I explained to the stewardess that an ambulance would be required upon arrival, that William was going into shock.

Death
inevitable
as sunset.

Still, he walks and
walks, somnambulist
of hope

His bright blood
pulsing like light
on a river
in morning.

═══

I called Betty last week and said, "Betty, I'm running like crazy, but I can't lose any weight."

"You eat too much," she said. "Why don't you give up drinking for a month, and then you'll get rid of some pounds."

These damn consultants. They always go right to the heart of the matter. But it is time to take a little stock, I guess.

This morning I tipped the scale at 211; a gut, yes, but I suck it in automatically when I run, and the rest of me is pretty chunky. My mother told me once she married my father because of his legs, tan, like palm tree trunks when he came back from Hawaii and the war. I guess tan legs were something of a rarity among the farmers and coal miners of western Pennsylvania.

I got his legs, anyhow, and my pecs and shoulder muscles would do for a Hathaway commercial. But damn the midsection. After thirty it's twice as hard to lose a pot. "Gravity's the enemy," William's old osteopath likes to say. "It will wear down even the ocean."

Have I completely capitulated to America's obsession with youth, turned into one of those bimbos who spend half their workout posing in front of the mirror at the gym? Is it wrong to look your age? Act your age? "We are always the same age inside," Gertrude Stein says. Character is what one looks for in a face. It's the flaw that accounts for the charm of a thing. . . . I can hear Betty keeping a stony silence.

I watched a documentary on aging recently that followed a seventy-five-year-old black woman in the days of her retirement. She runs five miles a day, looks half her age, keeps her life full of friends and volunteer work. "When I can't run anymore," she says, "why then, I'll walk." All you baby boomers out there had better watch out, the director seemed to be saying. If you make it to sixty-five, there's a good chance you'll make it to eighty-five, and being a successful senior citizen isn't just a matter of good genes and the luck of the Irish.

Lots of things are out of our control, fair enough. But that doesn't mean you trust everything to fate. You have to plan your emotional well-being as carefully as your financial security. If you're going to forgo children for a career, then you'd better develop some important friendships in your life, or your final years might turn out to be unbearably lonely. If you let yourself fall apart in middle age, you might spend the last twenty years of your life as an invalid parked in front of the TV at a nursing home. "Let's face it," William's osteopath once scolded me, "fat people just don't make it."

But what's more boring than dieting, except perhaps talking about dieting? Very simple really. Everyone knows all you have to do to lose weight is eat fewer calories and change your eating habits for the rest of your life. Right?

This morning's mail brought a CARE package from my sister Barbie. I had forgotten my T-shirt over the weekend when I went running with my brother-in-law (a canary-yellow singlet with a picture of Shakespeare flying in a Superman costume, a red S blazing on his chest). With the shirt she had included a back issue of *Runner's World* with articles on training. She also included a pound and a half of homemade peanut butter fudge. I almost fainted when I opened the box, and I can't even read the articles because the magazine still smells so wonderful. What an angel she is, savvy as Susan Sontag or Betty Friedan, but she would shrivel up if she couldn't bake cookies for the people she loves. An inherited trait, no doubt. When we unpacked our bags after the trip, my mother had included a loaf of banana nut bread and a quart of her special peach orange marmalade flecked with bits of ruby-red cherry. I can't stand it.

My problem is parties. Last night, for example, William and I went to the president's reception for the first faculty meeting of the year—President and Mrs. Ames are almost Chinese in their regard for emeritus professors, and William is always included in these events, like a distinguished family member. A hundred and fifty lovely, interesting people milling about, expectation almost

visible on the crisp September air. Somehow the best of intentions fly out the window when those cute boys and girls waltz up
to you with a big smile, a tray of mushroom caps stuffed with
crab, and a glass of Chivas Regal on the rocks. One drink and
that rosy good will takes over.

The lady across from you is ninety-two, wearing a blue enamel
daisy, laughing about the business courses she used to try to
teach the girls. She's riveting. The knockout young director of
development wants to know how you got your tan, and you can
feel yourself blush because her face is wide open with an honest
flirtation you haven't seen in years. One more scotch and I'll get
up the courage to meet the shy new professor in the corner who's
been following me around the party with his eyes. What a
beauty. Maybe he'll come with us for dinner. Where shall we
eat?

I've always tried to avoid taking on too much at once—like
dieting, stopping smoking, training for a marathon, and going
through a divorce—stress factors are cumulative. Trying to do
one hard thing makes trying to do another even more difficult.
Just common sense. But it seems I have to start on the weight
problem along with the discipline of running. Maybe I can start
off by eating my copy of *Runner's World.*

To balance the fudge, today's mail brought a letter from
Betty, who has become my coach. I guess our last conversation
made her think I really *am* going to try this run. Maybe she's just
feeling guilty for going off to Spain for a month, leaving me to
train on my own. Last week she had her son send me an entry
form for the Twenty-five-Kilometer Tune-Up Race in Central
Park on September 20. Just like a consultant. Let time work for
her. If I've really run the race by the time she comes back, she'll
know I'm serious and come visit us and run with me the way
she's been promising all summer. William and I thought if we
offered her two beautiful trees to plant on the overhang of her
new deck, that would be sufficient bait to get her up here. But
no, today's Dear John letter says she's leaving the country instead.

When we got into the terminal and the paramedics finally got an IV started, a cardiac monitor in place, and the stretcher ready for transport, incredibly we had to wait for somebody from the airline to bring a key for the elevator. My poor William lay there with a little smile, while we waited for some clerk to make his way to the gate. I got more and more agitated and was about to start screaming when the driver said, "The hell with this, this guy isn't going to make it," and we manhandled the stretcher down the escalator to the ambulance.

Sixteen hours after we arrived at the emergency room William underwent exploratory surgery. Of course, they found a ruptured appendix. We had waited hours for the various specialists to arrive to evaluate the case. The urologist was unable to insert a catheter and finally had to cut into the bladder from above. Since William had been on a blood thinner to prevent another stroke, the surgeon wouldn't operate until the clotting system worked sufficiently to keep him from bleeding to death. As time dragged on, William seemed to get more and more toxic as the infection began to take over his body.

I prayed that he would survive so that I would have a chance to be a better friend to him. All I wanted was to spend some happy years to make up for what we had been through. I promised myself once again I would read to him more often, prune trees and garden if he wanted, be more patient. If he only survived. I made my desperate little bargains with God the way I had done so often in the years since his heart problems and subsequent stroke.

I had been on the phone with William in Morocco when his heart first stopped. "I'm going away now," he said, and the phone went dead. Within forty-eight hours I had caught a plane home and was riding with him in the ambulance on the way to Yale Hospital for special cardiac care. Before he was even admitted the heart gave out again, and it took two hours to revive him. The permission form I signed for emergency surgery listed a 95 percent chance of mortality.

Until this appendectomy he had somehow managed to pull out of the worst. But he was rapidly using up his nine lives. A few days after the surgery it became clear that something was very wrong. The Cuban surgeon took me for a cup of coffee and explained that adhesions were blocking the intestines and William would require another operation. His heart was strong, though, and his able cardiologist assured me all would be well. At the end of six weeks, however, William had undergone five major operations, and the surgeon told me that if he didn't begin to respond after all this surgery, there was nothing more he could do.

William was pathetically thin, surviving on nutrients being fed through a tube in his neck. But in spite of all the torture of the past weeks, the starvation, the constant X-rays and barium studies, visits from the lab tech night and day to draw blood, and being stranded in a strange town with no friends, his spirits were miraculously good. The Cuban physicians were so kind to him. He was something of a legend in the hospital for his easy smile, blue eyes, and his unearthly patience. Nursing students wrote papers on his case, and found excuses to stop by to visit or bring some little gift. Most nights I would stay with him to be there in case he should have a seizure when no nurses were around, or if he was in pain. Otherwise, I went back to the little motel across the street from the hospital at the end of my day with him.

My life was a slow nightmare of boredom and cafeteria food, spiced with contrived optimism. The only thing that reduced the stress and took me out of myself a little were the morning runs before I went to the hospital. For a while I was able to forget a little, work up a sweat, and just look around at the strange barrio I was living in.

One day I happened to run into the Hialeah racetrack by accident. Hundreds of pink flamingos preened themselves or loitered in a shallow lake in the center of the track. Royal palms lined the entrance to the palatial clubhouse. The earth smelled fresh in the morning air. I stopped running and watched the horses come around the track, sleek creatures decked out in peacock colors. I had never seen anything so beautiful. I just stood there crying.

Sometimes as I ran, a phrase would come to me, or some image of the life of the hospital would take me over. There were lots of therapeutic meditations, like the "Nursing Triptych":

I

SECOND WIND, FLORIDA

On impulse, in 36 hours
we drove our colds to Miami.
Peeling the roof from the little
orange Porsche, the sour smells
of sickness and winter dissipated
in the heavy perfume of the orchards
as we decelerated into health.

Years later, I jog through
these same gardens before
my day begins at your bedside.

As I've grown to manhood it's clear
that any goodness I might aspire to
has been your doing. Even now,
your calm courage after
surgery is a seedling taking root
in my soul, threatened only by irony:

The bright music of the
ice cream truck, the warm
sunshine as I run barechest
are as odd as white funeral garb
in some exotic culture.

Cross country, alone by the mile
my orange blossom desperation.

II

CRUSTACEAN

Mr. Rivera, the roommate, is 88.
The tube from his throat gives off
white steam. He wears padded mittens.

When I raise my voice
in greeting, and place a hand
upon his arm, the tiny eyes
ignite. He pulls back his mittens
quicker than a sand crab darting
into a hole at the wave's edge.

The nurses call him Poppy and
plead with him not to struggle.
But finally they must catch him
and lash his mittens to the bed.

He rests, blows out steam,
the black beads mean and
full of scorn. As though
tying him down could stop
the ocean from crashing
against the shore, or snuff out
the bright star of his anger.

III

CARETAKER, LATE WATCH

He walks
the deserted square
of his heart

Where grief stalks
like a thief
in the shadows.

The dim moon
his only guide
clouds over

And the tower clock
strikes a single note
of remorse.

Love lately has
too much been
a holding action,

Death
inevitable
as sunset.

Still, he walks and
walks, somnambulist
of hope

His bright blood
pulsing like light
on a river
in morning.

I called Betty last week and said, "Betty, I'm running like crazy, but I can't lose any weight."

"You eat too much," she said. "Why don't you give up drinking for a month, and then you'll get rid of some pounds."

These damn consultants. They always go right to the heart of the matter. But it is time to take a little stock, I guess.

This morning I tipped the scale at 211; a gut, yes, but I suck it in automatically when I run, and the rest of me is pretty chunky. My mother told me once she married my father because of his legs, tan, like palm tree trunks when he came back from Hawaii and the war. I guess tan legs were something of a rarity among the farmers and coal miners of western Pennsylvania.

I got his legs, anyhow, and my pecs and shoulder muscles would do for a Hathaway commercial. But damn the midsection. After thirty it's twice as hard to lose a pot. "Gravity's the enemy," William's old osteopath likes to say. "It will wear down even the ocean."

Have I completely capitulated to America's obsession with youth, turned into one of those bimbos who spend half their workout posing in front of the mirror at the gym? Is it wrong to look your age? Act your age? "We are always the same age inside," Gertrude Stein says. Character is what one looks for in a face. It's the flaw that accounts for the charm of a thing. . . . I can hear Betty keeping a stony silence.

I watched a documentary on aging recently that followed a seventy-five-year-old black woman in the days of her retirement. She runs five miles a day, looks half her age, keeps her life full of friends and volunteer work. "When I can't run anymore," she says, "why then, I'll walk." All you baby boomers out there had better watch out, the director seemed to be saying. If you make it to sixty-five, there's a good chance you'll make it to eighty-five, and being a successful senior citizen isn't just a matter of good genes and the luck of the Irish.

Lots of things are out of our control, fair enough. But that
doesn't mean you trust everything to fate. You have to plan your
emotional well-being as carefully as your financial security. If
you're going to forgo children for a career, then you'd better
develop some important friendships in your life, or your final
years might turn out to be unbearably lonely. If you let yourself
fall apart in middle age, you might spend the last twenty years of
your life as an invalid parked in front of the TV at a nursing
home. "Let's face it," William's osteopath once scolded me,
"fat people just don't make it."

But what's more boring than dieting, except perhaps talking
about dieting? Very simple really. Everyone knows all you have
to do to lose weight is eat fewer calories and change your eating
habits for the rest of your life. Right?

This morning's mail brought a CARE package from my sister
Barbie. I had forgotten my T-shirt over the weekend when I
went running with my brother-in-law (a canary-yellow singlet
with a picture of Shakespeare flying in a Superman costume, a
red S blazing on his chest). With the shirt she had included a
back issue of *Runner's World* with articles on training. She
also included a pound and a half of homemade peanut butter
fudge. I almost fainted when I opened the box, and I can't even
read the articles because the magazine still smells so wonderful. What an angel she is, savvy as Susan Sontag or Betty
Friedan, but she would shrivel up if she couldn't bake cookies
for the people she loves. An inherited trait, no doubt. When
we unpacked our bags after the trip, my mother had included
a loaf of banana nut bread and a quart of her special peach
orange marmalade flecked with bits of ruby-red cherry. I can't
stand it.

My problem is parties. Last night, for example, William and I
went to the president's reception for the first faculty meeting of
the year—President and Mrs. Ames are almost Chinese in their
regard for emeritus professors, and William is always included in
these events, like a distinguished family member. A hundred and
fifty lovely, interesting people milling about, expectation almost

visible on the crisp September air. Somehow the best of intentions fly out the window when those cute boys and girls waltz up to you with a big smile, a tray of mushroom caps stuffed with crab, and a glass of Chivas Regal on the rocks. One drink and that rosy good will takes over.

The lady across from you is ninety-two, wearing a blue enamel daisy, laughing about the business courses she used to try to teach the girls. She's riveting. The knockout young director of development wants to know how you got your tan, and you can feel yourself blush because her face is wide open with an honest flirtation you haven't seen in years. One more scotch and I'll get up the courage to meet the shy new professor in the corner who's been following me around the party with his eyes. What a beauty. Maybe he'll come with us for dinner. Where shall we eat?

I've always tried to avoid taking on too much at once—like dieting, stopping smoking, training for a marathon, and going through a divorce—stress factors are cumulative. Trying to do one hard thing makes trying to do another even more difficult. Just common sense. But it seems I have to start on the weight problem along with the discipline of running. Maybe I can start off by eating my copy of *Runner's World.*

To balance the fudge, today's mail brought a letter from Betty, who has become my coach. I guess our last conversation made her think I really *am* going to try this run. Maybe she's just feeling guilty for going off to Spain for a month, leaving me to train on my own. Last week she had her son send me an entry form for the Twenty-five-Kilometer Tune-Up Race in Central Park on September 20. Just like a consultant. Let time work for her. If I've really run the race by the time she comes back, she'll know I'm serious and come visit us and run with me the way she's been promising all summer. William and I thought if we offered her two beautiful trees to plant on the overhang of her new deck, that would be sufficient bait to get her up here. But no, today's Dear John letter says she's leaving the country instead.

Dear Richard,

Here is some marathon advice:

Take the car and click off three separate three-mile tracks away from the house. Tie a ribbon on the tree or mark it with a stone. Then, every day, you run a different run, three miles out and three miles back (sixty minutes). Or (forty minutes) two miles out and two back, on the four-mile days. There's nothing as monotonous as repeating the same circuit to get your mileage.

In the month of September, when the schedule calls for the long run—do half of it in the morning and the other half in the afternoon. Then in October you can put them together IF your weight is down.

And that's the most important advice—get rid of ten or fifteen pounds as fast as you can. Just cut down on the food, because the running doesn't make that much difference. Take off a half pound a day until you feel about right, and you'll see a great difference in the effort it takes to do the mileage. I'm serious, now, you shouldn't be running at all if you haven't got the weight off. It's like running with a small steamer trunk on your head!

Do go up to New York alone and run in the park with the pack. You'll really get a joyful kick out of it and meet a lot of people your age.

I'll be thinking about you as I wind up and down the Mallorcan hills.

Affectionately,
Betty

How often between now and race day will I have to rededicate myself to this project? Happily, I have kept mostly on target for running, but the holidays have been murder on the diet, and the extra weight still has me working twice as hard as I need to do to get up those hills. I'm also beginning to appreciate hazards other than the boredom, illness, pain, drinking too much, and bad weather that could keep me from training successfully.

Instead of decreasing the stress in your life, training often increases stress as your distances get longer and you have to find more and more time in the day for running. This means less time for writing, paying the bills, preparing the meals, working with William on speech and physical therapy, and all the little chores that eat up the day. And the extra demands you're making on your body in training require more sleep, so getting up earlier doesn't work.

The only thing William can really do on his own that he likes is gardening, but already this summer we've had a number of trips to the emergency room after I've tried letting him work on his own. After he's had his shower and breakfast I've got to be at least within earshot for the rest of the day. Yesterday he didn't answer my call, and I found him standing precariously on the hill in front of the house, saw in hand, trying to take down a small tree that was crowding out the rock garden. I cut it down in two seconds and then realized that instead of helping, all I'd done was point out his limitations to him once again. His great pride is that he is not allergic to poison ivy, and he goes around fearlessly pulling it out with his bare hands. He used to shock and amaze guests in the old days by walking the grounds and pulling out piles of it as it crept out of the woods. Friends would call him up to see if he had a free afternoon to work at their house just rooting it out. Once after such an expedition he came home and inadvertently patted me on the back. The next day I was marked with the perfect shape of his palm etched in poison ivy.

Friends and colleagues from the old days at the college come by for an hour or so during the week, and that helps a little. After his stroke I tried to enlist all of William's friends to read with him and study as Roald Dahl did for Patricia Neal after her stroke. There wasn't much in the way of therapy in those days, and Dahl simply invented a program of his own using volunteers. Right after her stroke neighbors began to tutor her in the fundamentals of reading, writing, arithmetic, as though she were just beginning grade school. Anything that might stimulate speech and keep her spirit engaged was worth a try. Though professional therapists now worry a little about possible harm from such untrained volunteers, it seems to me that *any* human contact made in good faith has to be beneficial, unless the volunteer acts like a drill sergeant and starts pushing the patient around. Dahl's system remains the basis of certain therapy programs in England to this day, though he and Neal have long since divorced.

A few friends have stuck with William's program over the years, and the progress he's made is due to that sort of consistency. When he first had his stroke he couldn't say a single word and was completely paralyzed on the right side of his body. After years of very hard physical therapy he now walks just fine. We have lifetime memberships at the local spa, and he swims like a porpoise. But William can't write or read more than newspaper headlines, though he does understand everything he *hears.* He has minimal language to make himself sufficiently understood most of the time for basic needs. But that this great poet whose whole life was language should suffer from expressive aphasia, that his soul should be held hostage by his own damaged body, is an irony I can hardly imagine sometimes. In the early years after his stroke we were taking a little vacation in San Juan when his situation first became really clear to me.

APHASIA

Your face brightens
watching the delivery truck
navigate the tiny
labyrinth of Old San Juan.

It tries another approach,
backs down the street
out of my view. But
the dilemma continues,
reflected in the
glass doors of the café.

From where you sit
I suppose you see the driver
throw up his hands and
curse the horns blowing
behind him. Are they
blowing so angrily at him?

You watch the bemused
pedestrians perhaps, or a
cop who stops flirting
with the sweet brown girl
and wanders over to do his duty.

I can only see
flashes of truck headlights,
a girl's blue blouse, a
policeman waving his arm—
the event only shattered
pieces dropped into the end
of a kaleidoscope.

The tables have turned:
I'm the one who must
piece the shards together,
imagine reality from
broken reflections.
I see the enormity of your
courage and close my eyes.

If there is one thing I've learned about taking care of William
after his stroke, it's that things take time. I saw a poster once
with the ocean crashing against the cliffs and the simple message
below: Things take time. It may not sound like an astounding
insight, but if families could only appreciate this fact in the

soul-crushing first few months after a loved one has had a stroke, the situation wouldn't seem so hopeless. A corollary platitude I could offer is that the grueling work of rehabilitation is *worth* it. The day after you've smashed up your new Porsche and your nose and maybe an arm or two and your head is throbbing and there's the law to deal with and your eyes look like purple plums or the mask on a raccoon, you might think it better if the ambulance had never found you wrapped around that telephone pole. But in weeks or maybe months things begin to heal, maybe never perfectly, maybe with nasty scar tissue, but at least you're still in the ball game and there's hope of moving on to better days. At my birthday party three weeks ago William stood up and gave me a simple, beautiful toast. The pretty girl sitting beside him was moved to tears. The rum cake was enough to make you faint.

When you begin to look after someone who has had a stroke, it seems impossible that anything will ever change. Everything the patient does takes forever to accomplish. Tying his or her shoes becomes a triumph of independence, but may require an hour to achieve. Every detail of his or her waking life is negotiated at turtle speed. And when you live in close to a person with a handicap, it is as easy to appreciate progress as to watch your hair grow out. But if you can develop patience and appreciate the long haul, one day, a number of years later, you and your friend sit on a deck sipping Campari as the big ship pulls into some aquamarine bay in the Caribbean. You're tan, well dressed, and looking forward to lobster. Maybe it isn't living happily ever after, but the pleasure of life at least doesn't have to disappear from the horizon forever just because of a stroke.

Even under normal circumstances, though, once a person retires from academic life he might as well have died or gone to live in Wyoming. Academic politics are too intense to accommodate those without power. Life in the slow lane isn't where it's at when you're breaking the speed limit to get tenure, or the Pulitzer, the department chairmanship, or the chairman's wife. Cynicism can eat you up when the support you get from people you'd expect to help is polite and mostly token. The person responsible for the care has to be realistic too about what to expect from friends. People live very busy lives, what can you say? You can't really blame anyone.

Some individuals raise children, write novels, take care of an aging parent, keep a house, and maintain a husband. My lot seems pretty insignificant by comparison, I suppose, but I feel burdened at times. The key is to keep from feeling resentment or self-pity. You've got to treat yourself every now and then, take a vacation, eat a Dove Bar, run a marathon.

But were the old days any less hectic with each of us trying to maintain a career, and keep our love alive long distance? When we were far from each other for too long, the mail invariably brought a note like this one:

A HALF-YEAR COME AND GONE

In the hours it takes to turn the world
half over, you pried the heart
out of a warm grey chest.
I missed it all September.

Since when
the world has tilted north again,
while we kept warm together in
cycles of our own turning.
I tell you, keep the heart.

Halfway, halfway in a happy year
I tell you I can't remember
a prettier half-reversal of this sphere.

Our life has always been very social, a busy life filled with travel and many friends. Each of us came to his sexuality before Stonewall, and neither of us is particularly political or feels it necessary to declare his "sexual orientation." Unenlightened, perhaps, but more a question of aesthetics, I think, for each of us. I've never felt comfortable with the easy flirtation and high-pitched familiarity of gay bars, for example, though I keep returning to them like someone afraid of heights who forces himself to take the elevator every day. Neither of us is afraid to fight for civil rights when that's needed, but our own friendship has always been a very private affair, and William's illness has reinforced that "life-style," as people say today.

Last winter a stupid commercial on television combined a line from a popular song, "I haven't got time for the pain," with shots of people returning to hard physical jobs sufficiently relieved of arthritis pain or a headache by taking Tylenol or Bayer Aspirin. William and I happened to get a wicked flu about that time and felt just awful. We simply went to bed and didn't get up, except to eat, for four days. "William, baby," I said, when the commercial came on the TV at the foot of the bed, "we've got time for the pain."

When I go to a new town and decide to jog around on my own I'm always amazed how much more I see than if I had zoomed around on the tour bus. People in a hurry don't live very long. Repeat one hundred times slowly, Richard. People in a hurry don't live very long.

One thing you don't count on when you begin to run is the animosity you sometimes encounter from different quarters. A certain kind of motorist might blast his horn just to see if he can make you jump out of your skin, like Buffalo Bill using bison for target practice. It's easier to understand someone who comes wheeling around the corner too fast and is so scared by the fact that he almost creamed you that he lets off a little steam by shouting you off the road. But it's a blow when some obese character on your left at a dinner party blows smoke in your face and speculates that you just aren't getting enough sex, that it is unnatural and bad for your health to try to run twenty-six miles.

In the beginning you keep your aspirations to self-improvement a secret lest you seem self-righteous in the not-so-charming vein of a reformed smoker. And, as my father is fond of saying, "You can always say what you've done, not what you're going to do." You're setting yourself up to eat a very large crow if you don't happen to finish the marathon. But, boy, it's hard to keep from letting anyone know when you finally have run one of the Sunday long runs of twelve or fifteen miles during training.

When I was first fanning myself out into the peacock strut college freshmen perform when they are getting the lay of the land, I challenged a kid in the dorm to a footrace. He'd been bragging about his speed and how sure he was that he'd make first string on the intramural soccer team. I was a lot thinner then, and fast, and I knew I could beat him in the short run. All our friends lined up at the track, bets were placed, and bam, we were off. I turned out to be so out of shape I couldn't even sprint around the track once. Classmates still occasionally ask me if I've challenged anyone to a race lately.

Well, today, praise Allah, I ran 12.8 miles up and down these hills without stopping, and I feel like writing the Georgetown alumni magazine to put out the good word. Throughout the week I managed to follow the schedule for the first time, running a total of 28 miles by Saturday. I had only two drinks last night, went to bed early, and slept until ten. When I woke up I knew this was the day.

The greatest danger for a marathon runner is dehydration and heat exhaustion. Runners' magazines all give first aid advice on tackling a runner who is struggling on blindly, clearly in trouble, but out of his head with determination to finish. Such runners can die very quickly if they aren't stopped and their body temperature brought down. The manuals are full of instructions on training yourself to replace body fluids during the long runs— and how to control your bladder too, it turns out. So this morning I dutifully set out three plastic glasses of water in the mailbox and prepared to run around the loop four times, 3.2 miles per loop.

The past couple of weeks my feet have been so exquisitely sensitive to the pavement it's as though I were running in my bedroom slippers and could feel every pebble like the princess and the pea. I decided to prepare for my first big run Saturday afternoon by buying a new pair of shoes. The tread doesn't wear out as fast as the supporting structures do in running shoes, especially when 210 pounds come crashing down on those supports every step you take. But when I put on my new Sauconys it was like slipping into springy stilts. My feet had a life of their own.

I applied Vaseline between my thighs and on my privates to avoid the chafing that had begun to bother me at the end of the longer runs. With a sweaty shirt rubbing you over the miles, even the nipples sometimes get worn raw. Lots of runners cover them with Band-Aids, which is a little shocking when they take off their shirts at a race. It was still cool enough, though, to run shirtless this morning and avoid that particular problem. The leaves were just beginning to turn yellow, peach, and scarlet. I put on my headphones and tuned in to "Morning Pro Musica." They had scheduled a program of all Mozart. If there was ever a morning to make it around the course four times, this was it.

Some say the most important thing a runner can do to avoid shinsplints, pulled ligaments, and stress fractures is to warm up the body first with a series of exercises, especially knee bends and stretching the Achilles tendon. I prefer the new "expert" thinking, which says it's better to warm up by just jogging slowly when you begin to run. I can only make myself do the bare minimum when I think about a run the first thing in the morning. The older I get the stiffer I am when I wake up, and starting my warm-up is as easy as turning over a weak battery in subzero weather. I prefer to warm up by starting out very slowly and jogging the stiffness out.

Throughout the race, they say, your pace should be comfortable enough to talk without getting out of breath. Since I don't have anyone to run with here in the country, this translates into singing along with a favorite song on the radio headset, though the melody is pretty staccato and high-pitched when you try to sing and run at the same time.

After I ran the first loop this morning I stopped at the mailbox to have a pee and drink the first glass of water I had stashed there. Wonderful relief on both counts. I couldn't believe I had been running without replacing fluids up till now. One little glass of water was like taking a shower and for a short while left me as fresh as when I had started.

At the end of the second loop, as far as I had ever run in my training to date, I was tired but elated to be on the home stretch. First I had to negotiate Ryan's Hill, however, a little monster two hundred yards long that would come to a plateau ever so slightly before shooting straight up to the next height. "Isn't this a sweet hill, Uncle Rich?" my nephew would say with a grin when we came across such a killer during our runs together last summer. Nice. Cocky and charming. It isn't all orange Mohawks and nasty beastie boys in his generation.

When I got to the top of sweet Ryan for the fourth time, fully conscious of the effort to bring up each lead piston once again, I knew I would finish the course no matter what I might think later. I was two hours into the run, Mozart had been replaced by my old friend, Susan Stamberg's "Weekend Edition," and the hubbub of the pope's coming visit took my mind off how hot it had become in the noonday sun.

The popemobile would take him through eight major cities,

each targeted to reflect special concerns of groups within the Church. Already one could buy Pope on a Rope Soap, or a hand-painted John Paul II water sprinkler (Let Us Spray). And this morning before the pope got on *Shepherd I* the Vatican fired a dramatic shot across the bow of the American Catholic Church by declaring that Catholics had no right to pick and choose the items of doctrine they decided to believe in. The old sadness washed over me again. That this beautiful and obviously holy man should be such an unfortunate reactionary, especially after the hope one felt with John XXIII, is, is what, disheartening? The world is dying of starvation from overpopulation and the Church condemns birth control. Couples desperate to have children try to live a full married life by using modern reproductive technology and do so under a moral cloud. What instinct is at work in such couples except generosity and self-sacrifice? Can't we protect against the dangers of genetic engineering, preserve the dignity of human life, and still offer some options to such couples? And what of people who share their lives and express love for one another even though they are of the same sex, perhaps ten or fifteen million such people in America alone? Can they all be living a life of mortal sin?

In some gay rag recently the editorialist encouraged us to send a card to the Vatican asking the Pope to please stay home. I described this proposition to my brother, and he was fairly shocked. He said the Church was striving for universality, an appeal throughout the world and not only to the particular concerns of American Catholics. He is pained by some of the Church's decisions and is trying to be generous and understanding. Faithful. But he's always given me his unqualified love and support as I have made my way in the world and explored my sexual identity.

My brother spent a number of years in the seminary before he married, the Benedictine order. He and his wife had four children, and then they adopted five more of various races—a kind of little UN or monastery of their own.

He's a bright man, a loving man. He lives one of the most spiritual lives I know of but is not naive about the world. I love

him, and I am so proud of him and his wonderful wife Janie for
the beautiful family life they have created. But it is difficult to
explain to less charitable if well-meaning Catholics what it does
to you when the love that has given your whole life value most of
your adult years is considered evil or at least contemptible by
your church.

You don't want to be sniveling about it. It takes most gays
many years to feel comfortable with themselves, to overcome the
bitterness that consumed their younger days and get on with the
business of their lives. But invariably they find someone to love,
do their work, deal with the daily problems of life as best they
can just like anyone else. Many find it easier just to give up on
the Church and its condemnation and go their own way. Others
aspire to a spiritual life, a ritual of celebration, a vehicle to bring
meaning and some sort of moral idealism or shape to their lives.
Some gay Catholics live a kind of divine loneliness, a spiritual
isolation that has nothing to do with fear of hell or damnation.

I'm always saddened when I think of the Church's unyielding
position on homosexuality. William and I still have sex, filled
with love and gentle, even fairly athletic, pleasure. We've shared
a lot of years together, and I'm praying for a lot more. He looks
great, dresses elegantly. He carries himself before guests or the
public with dignity. Even on those days when there's a certain
fragility in his uprightness, he makes my heart swell. And he still
has a wonderful sense of humor.

Sometimes at night when he threatens a seizure or has some
new pain I stay awake the whole night and watch to see if he
develops a fever, if the medications will prove to be insufficient,
if some new mystery of caring for this dear old guy is in store for
me. It's very hard sometimes, not knowing what will come next.
But I love him, and if he has the courage to face it, I'll try to do
whatever my energy will finally enable me to do. This hardly
makes me Mother Teresa. People routinely look after one another when life gets tough, regardless of their sex. Most of the
caregiving in this country still happens outside the nursing
home. But at this point in my life with William I certainly don't
plan to give up sex to satisfy the Church's notion of proper moral

conduct. He wouldn't make it without me; at least I tell myself I'm needed this way, the way anyone does who is in love.

One can't sin against one's own blood, one's conscience—it has nothing to do with picking and choosing those doctrines one would like to adhere to. The Catholic Church has to be something more than a grid against which the life of the spirit is tested, mere pontification. The country is praying for a theology to help us live better lives in the face of difficult and complex questions, some of which have never been faced before. It needs the revolutionary love that Christ brought to the Church initially. In San Francisco they have decided to pray for the pope, not with him.

My old friend Martha gave me a thank-you gift last week at dinner, a cobalt-blue inkwell—nineteenth century and very pretty—for the trouble of delivering ninety gallons of water every other day throughout the summer when her well went dry. Martha likes to tweak my nose occasionally about my pretensions of being a Catholic, and reminded me that Martin Luther wound up throwing *his* inkwell at the devil. I'm keeping her gift on the windowsill to spite her. The afternoon sun illuminates the glass and casts a ray of deep blue light like hope across my desk, which cheers me quite a lot.

Labor Day is always such a bittersweet holiday for me. Whatever fireworks display I ever watched as a kid, it couldn't obviate the fact that tomorrow school started, that bareback weather was over, that it was time to come indoors like the field mice and crickets. To reinforce the lesson, it always seemed to rain just as the fireworks were about to end. No more corn on the cob, no more blueberries or peaches for another year.

Families invariably have a final barbecue to take stock of how things are and say goodbye to summer. I guess I don't know anyone who uses this occasion to celebrate the number of Ford station wagons they helped roll off the production line, or the number of insurance policies they sold that year. It's a time to lick your wounds a little, and take a last walk on the beach with someone you love. It is not like May Day in Moscow. But it does make you think about where you're going as the wind begins to grow colder.

I suppose I should be proud of the work I do making a life for me and William, and I am. But though it is a full-time job, taking care of a person who has a disability, it's not really considered work in our society. It's just something that is supposed to get accomplished, usually by the eldest daughter in the family, in the process of doing all the other things one does in life like earning a living and raising children. We spent close to $50,000 on nursing care—or the insurance did—the first year I couldn't leave my work to take care of William. I had to travel so much with my job, setting up health care programs for expatriate personnel, we simply had to hire nurses. So it's not as though I'm unaware of the value in the work. Some wise legislators realize that the financial burden of such care will become a national crisis as the population increases.

I dutifully threw a barbecue, though, to thank certain friends for their help during the summer and to entertain an old high school classmate and his family. One of his daughters was thinking about going to school in New England, and they wished to stop by our college over the Labor Day weekend.

The daughter he brought along was as beautiful as his other children, if a little too flashy with her long red nails and gold bracelets. She had just returned from a summer vacation in Europe with friends. She wasn't sure what she wanted to study in college, she only knew she intended to make a lot of money to "maintain her life-style" or become a spy.

I thought of the young woman I had heard debating one of the founders of the feminist movement on TV recently, who argued that the woman of the eighties was interested in looking good and having a stable relationship. Nostalgia for the fifties went deeper than a love for rock and roll. The beautiful dolly implied that women today really wanted to be sexy cookie-bakers again, that the feminist movement of the sixties was somehow only a quaint blip on the historical oscilloscope, like tie-dyed clothes or a beehive hairdo. The old feminist just dropped her jaw and watched thirty years of work for the liberation of future sisters go up in smoke, as though the Stepford wives had all risen from the grave, joined the Young Republicans Club, and were holding a fashion show to benefit Shoppers' Rights.

My friend's daughter wasn't quite this hard-core, but I had to wonder if the pursuit of one's life-style wasn't a bit limited a goal for someone just starting out in the world. With a CEO's level-headedness, and because he was so proud of her beauty, her father just winked at me and let the silliness pass. He was aware that reality has a way of crashing down on us, setting us straight quite soon enough in life. There was no need to rush it. He clearly didn't plan to spoil her forever. And she *had* earned her own air fare to Europe that summer after all.

The girl was just the sort of long-stemmed American rose that had caused me so many problems when I was going to college, except that this scarlet-haired creature could have been my daughter. I was feeling a little dated by the end of supper.

Certainly a lot of my generation joined the Peace Corps to

beat the draft or get a foot in the foreign service door. But we always felt the need for at least the pretense of some sort of idealism when we talked about our lives. Ronald Reagan had legitimized the "creed of greed," Toyota sold cars by "looking out for number one," popular films talked of earning money the *really* old-fashioned way, inheriting it, and television ran such hit programs as "Lifestyles of the Rich and Famous."

"Oh my hippie soul," I said, wringing my hands just as my parents might have done as I stormed out of the house to smoke pot and plot the revolution with friends. At least this generation was just saying no to drugs.

When I was in high school my birthday fell on the first day of football training. I couldn't sleep the night before my birthday because I knew that for the next three weeks I would be too stiff to move at the end of each sweltering day of practice. It became a game of how much lemonade you could drink and throw up during the midday break lying around under the trees. By Labor Day, though, you were hard, the weather was cool, and your photograph was being taken for the programs that would be distributed throughout the season. I went back to York to visit my family this summer and happened to be running around the track the day photos were being taken for this year's team. My God, how young they all looked as they knelt on one knee clutching a football, laughing at the wisecracks their teammates made to keep them from looking properly tough. It looked like a grade school team, not high school. Could I ever have looked that young? Would the fact that the young looked young ever be something to consider?

Some of the football players sported blond Mohawk haircuts—Coach Sinkovitz would never have let us try that. One boy actually wore an earring. Each time around the track I knocked off one of the thirty pebbles I had lined up to count the laps I needed to make for the day's run, and I gradually became soaked with sweat in the sun. I kept hoping someone would throw me a ball or at least make a catcall. Then I remembered that when I had played football sometimes runners would come out to use our field. They looked like old college athletes, thirty, maybe even forty years old. They were big and chunky, and you didn't fuck around with them. They were men. I ran around the track in silence until there were no more pebbles left, then I jogged home alone.

The last stretch of the loop I run here on the river is my favorite, and not just because I'm coming home at that point in the run. Trees shade the road most of the way, producing a wonderful lime-green light, and there's always a breeze coming off the river to cool me down. A black squirrel usually runs with me for twenty or thirty yards until he shoots off into the woods. For some reason we rarely meet a car back there, so I can jog right down the middle of the road, which is flat and runs along a tall cornfield stretching out to the river. Once, feeling a little isolated by this life in the country taking care of William, I remembered the line from Keats where Ruth, "sick for home, stood in tears amid the alien corn." This morning, like magic, the cornfield was gone, ploughed under by a farmer cutting his losses after the summer's drought.

When I came to my favorite stretch of the road this morning, the river was silver and boiling. But the closer I came to the river, the closer I came to throwing up with the feculent smell of fish kill. Hundreds, perhaps thousands, of fish were flopping lethargically on the surface of the water, and the shore was smeared with dead fish half rotted and pecked apart by the gulls.

Neighbors are very nonchalant about the phenomenon, consider it just part of nature. People say that by the end of summer the oxygen content has grown very low. They explain that schools of smaller fish suffocate when the bluefish chase them into shallow water.

No one seems to care about *why* all this dead water is coming to us from the Long Island Sound. For years New York has been dumping its sewage sludge into the ocean where the tide theoretically washes it away, but instead, the tide often just washes it right back, I've read, with needles, pills, vials of blood. The algae grow so thick on the sludge that the water is brown soup by the end of summer, and sometimes old condoms and feces wash up on the beach.

New home builders now tend to put in swimming pools by the

water's edge for the view. Our towns are coming to resemble a cheap science fiction world where cities can only be sustained if they are built under plastic domes. I swim a lot less at the local beaches by the end of summer. Even the jellyfish that usually float in to ruin the swimming by the end of August seem to have been killed off this year. Beach closings these days don't mean a great white shark, they mean the risk of infection or disease if you swim in the filthy water. Niantic Bay scallops, the epicure's delicacy, have disappeared from the bay. And now even the poor dolphins are suffering from some AIDS-like disease plaguing the ocean that attacks their immune system. Possibly a vibrio organism, like the one causing cholera.

I've never been a particularly fervent environmentalist, but now I ran by the stubbled cornfield grieving for the foul end-of-summer river and the beautiful creatures I'd seen on TV washing ashore, pockmarked, rotting, innocent.

THE DOLPHINS

Who hasn't
at some point
succumbed.
Their sleek
intelligence
their wit.
The charm of a
boy on a dolphin.

Since men first tried
the dark oceans,
these silver animals
have burst into the blue air
unexpected as friendship.
And lonely sailor boys
might strip to imitate
the sport these brothers took
in each other's shining bodies.

In dark caves
behind the bars
pretty boys
beautiful men
still swim in their
pleasure like dolphins
at death in the seas.

Nothing avails
their animal innocence.
Extinction is the
unnatural act.

The dolphin's song
fades like the ocean
noise trapped
in a conch shell, the last
shy smile of a boy
drowned at sea.

This past summer I got a letter that began, "Dear Mrs. Meredith: We are pleased to inform you that you have *already won* one of the fabulous prizes listed below." All I had to do it seemed was to come and collect my prize after taking a no-obligation tour of the time-sharing resort they were pleased to offer. As I recall, the prize list included such items as a new Thunderbird, a Caribbean cruise for two, a full-length black diamond mink coat, and a Kodak camera. I wondered what the chances were that I had *not* won a Kodak camera, a very *small* Kodak camera.

But the resort was located on Long Island Sound only forty-five minutes away, and if nothing else it might be a nice drive, I thought. Several agonizing hours later a good old boy from Georgia had relieved us of $20,000 for two weeks' ownership at the Sound Paradise and a permanent gold card membership in the sports facility that would be built one day west of the hotel under construction. The restaurant was to be rated five stars, and who knew how high the value on such property might climb? Kate Hepburn and Art Carney lived *practically* down the street. We were virtually *stealing* our two weeks at that price, in fact the unit we wanted had been reserved for the manager, but the salesman felt honor bound to stick by his commitment.

I'd like to say it was all William's doing, but I did finally sign the check, I guess. It *might* be nice to meet friends at the little train station in the village—"About as quaint as you can get in southeastern Connecticut," the salesman reminded us—and take them for a nice lunch and swim before driving home. The sports facility would be like a private gym for William's physical therapy. The resort would be deserted and peaceful after Labor Day.

I installed William in the little golf car shuttle back to the parking lot. The Kodak was an eight-millimeter movie camera, the kind your father used to use to catch you trying out your new hula hoop. In an age of videotape, it was the Edsel of the camera world.

For a couple of days now we've been installed at the Sound Paradise, and though the front desk is still quite disorganized, it has been a nice change of pace running through the little seaside villages. Many of the houses are eighteenth century, William's favorite period of architecture—philosophy too, for that matter. There are antique shops to tempt the tourist every quarter mile or so along the main road. There are old-fashioned barbershops, clam bars, vegetable and fruit stands—enough local color to inspire a lifetime supply of *New Yorker* covers. The weather is uncertain now, and each morning when I wake up it is likely that gray skies will have covered us over and the first of the fall rains will have come. Once you have gotten your body heat up, though, running in the rain is kind of fun. You're not supposed to run in the rain, of course, riskier terrain and dangerous, but if a runner stayed out of the rain, he'd never complete his training.

Last Sunday I missed the last mass at the local church by the time I got up, and so I decided I would let a really long run serve as my religious duty for the day. When I went out to buy milk and breakfast things for William I took along several bottles of water and stashed them along the route I planned to run. It was just six miles to the dock where all the yachts tie up and the rich folks arrive to eat in the fancy restaurants. I hid a bottle of seltzer at the two- and four-mile points so I would have water coming and going along what would be a twelve-mile run. Just as I got William installed with breakfast in front of "Meet the Press" with promises to hold off on his shower until I returned from my run, the skies opened up with a fairly heavy rain.

At first inside my red slicker I was dry as a bug in an Aubusson. Mahler was working his way to a symphonic triumph. I could have been listening to the music sitting on the deck back at the condominium just staring out at the ocean. The harder it rained, though, the more water gathered by the roadside. There was little room for passing cars, and soon my bare legs and shorts were soaked by cars throwing up waves of dirty water as they drove by. My shoes filled and squished out like a sponge every time I came down on them. The little cave of my slicker was hot and humid now, but it was too cold to strip down. At the four-

mile mark I slipped into a large stand of pine trees lining someone's yard where I had stashed my water bottle. I had a long
drink and a long pee, then headed back into the rain.

Before coming to the dock I ran by beautiful marsh grasses
that grew higher than my head. It was like running along the
Nile. When I reached the dock it was deserted. Only a few wild
swans and one brave skipper plowed through the choppy gray
waves. Initially the rain was refreshing and made the run easier.
Now, the run home would be a great relief knowing that every
step I took would be taking me home. The humidity bothered
the ankle I had broken all those years ago in Switzerland. It had
become a good gauge of the weather just the way it's supposed to
work for old folks.

When I finally limped up to the porch back at Paradise, William had had his shower, of course. But fortunately he hadn't
slipped. It's a bore for him, I know, to have to have someone's
"permission" to manage the routine activities of his life, but the
shower stall is "the enemy," I keep telling him. If he ever falls
and hits his head, we might not get a hemorrhage stopped, with
all the blood thinners he's on. But who can blame him for saying
to hell with it from time to time?

I could tell from the smell that he hadn't opened the damper
at first when he started a fire in the fireplace. Fortunately he
hadn't set off the smoke alarm, and once he had the damper
figured out he had laid out a beautiful fire. I stood close to the
flames trying to get the goose bumps off my legs. I held my
breath as he carried a steaming mug of coffee across the room to
me, another surprise he'd cooked up to welcome me back from
my run.

"Thank you, honey," I said. "This is about the best coffee in
the world." And I meant it.

Tomorrow it will be just a month since I started this project, and amazingly I am still with it. They say if you make it through the first month of your training, past your first big run, you'll make it. By the end of that time you'll have made running a routine and discovered a way to arrange your life around your daily runs.

All the articles on running agree that the longer runs become more important as you progress. "That's what distance running is," Bill Squires says in *Runner's World:* "The body against the course, the growing number of miles and the increasing fatigue. This natural erosion of the body's resources is all that should concern you during the race. Learn how it feels, how it descends on you and how to tolerate it. Accomplish this and you will finish the marathon, because your training in the next two months will greatly extend your body's resistance."

Just be concerned about the natural erosion of the body's resources, he says, as though one could be preoccupied with anything else. Tomorrow the spirit of Betty Lussier will be lecturing me long distance about erosion as I traipse around Central Park trying to run the Twenty-five-Kilometer Tune-Up Race she's pushed me into.

The Amtrak car I'm riding in is quite warm, makes me feel very snug against the gray rainy weather outside as we chug down to New York. The somber beauty of New England in the fall.

"After it rains, it gets cold," a little retarded boy informed me in the train station. He liked the baseball cap I was wearing. Why didn't I give it to him?

The boats are all moored, the beaches are empty. Two saints—Cosmas and Damian?—stand together in the cold in front of a Catholic Church we pass by. The American flag someone has attached to Damian's staff snaps out straight in the wind. Even the swans seem forlorn bobbing around in the black water beyond the marsh grasses. Nature knows winter is coming and is saddened by the fact. Pathetic fallacy? We project our emotions into the dead matter of the world. Are these swans warning me to stay home?

I'm breaking one of the rules twice today. All the guides warn you not to run races on your training days, but how could I resist this morning's third annual Road Race sponsored by the Downtown New London Association?

Months ago I kept a nice young jeweler after hours engraving a dog tag for Mikey. We were on our way out of town and needed some sort of ID should he run away while were gone. I told the jeweler as he worked that I planned to treat myself to a really good emerald earring if I lost thirty pounds and finished the marathon. My parents won't let me in the house, of course, if I come home with an emerald earring, and I doubt I'll get thin enough in the face to where it might look good. George Michael I am not. But I've always wondered what I might look like, and it's not as though I'm indulging a desire to smoke crack or parade around on a dog leash for some character dressed in leather.

The jeweler showed me a few stones—the clearer they are, the more sparkle, the more expensive. Then he gave me an application for today's run. The merchants have sponsored it for three years now to attract people to a failing inner-city shopping area. Same old story; all the suburbanites flock to the Crystal Mall or order through the fancy mail-order catalogs. None of the chichi stores in the mall would have stayed open late to engrave a dog tag for Mikey the way Malloves Jewelers was willing to do. I felt I owed it to the seedy strip of sailor bars, record shops, and little restaurants that made up greater downtown New London to enter the race. Five miles, flat and fast, just a mile short of what I'm scheduled to run in my training schedule for today anyway. Why not run it just for fun to prepare for tomorrow's Twenty-five-Kilometer Tune-Up?

It was difficult to leave Jimmy Merrill's dinner party last night to go to bed early for this morning's race. "Just a few of 'the boys,' " he had said when he invited us. It was bound to be lively.

Talk centered mostly on the good old days in Greece. One guest recalled all the CIA projects funded with leftover monies from World War II. There were stories of lovers' quarrels ending in murder and outrageous gossip about porno stars of the 1930s. Someone recounted yet *another* indignity the long-suffering token duchess has had to endure in the heat of village social life. Standard Stonington fare.

It's hard sometimes not to be a little jealous when I'm around James Merrill. I tend to ruminate on how unfair life can be, turn over the past in my mind. "Look at him," my lesser self whines, "rich as Donald Trump, houses in various corners of the world, at the very peak of his considerable career, winner of every award known to civilized man." I think of all the years William worked with students, each life a poem in its own right, and still found time to create his own extraordinary poems—little gems of technical brilliance and moral clarity. Yet William's work remains fairly unknown in our culture, is less fashionable.

We watched a program on public television last night documenting the life of Truman Capote, an "American Master." Here's a man of such decadence and squalor you can hardly bear to watch him, a man who wasted his talent over decades of self-indulgence, presented to us as the troubled genius of his times. And what is the masterpiece? An obsessional report of butcherlike murders in the Midwest, blurring the line between journalism and snuff films, designed to titillate us and sell books—whew! I sound more righteous than brother Jimmy Swaggart.

But ever since I began thinking about the question seriously in graduate school, I could never see the distinction between an artist's life and his work. My hippie aesthetics always chose Shelley over Byron, for example, no matter what the professor said, because Shelley lived what he believed. Byron was a cad, and funny, and probably better technically, but in those naive days we went to poetry for truth as much as for beauty. If poets didn't have an inside track on what life was all about, who did?

William's work has its loyal following, his stock continues to rise and will certainly outlive the present gurus of literary taste. But I'm like an aggressive wife, I guess, anxious for the recognition her mate deserves. William would think me funny, chide me for being small-minded. He might even point out that I'm as gossipy and bitchy as Truman Capote myself on occasion. Several more lives on the wheel for me, no doubt, before I spin off into nirvana.

Anyhow, getting up this morning at 7:30 after last night's party wasn't easy, and William was extremely sweet about it all. Years ago I always used to lie abed while he got the house warmed up and coffee started at the crack of dawn. Pilgrim Airlines had a little commuter flight back to D.C. that would have me teaching my first class by 9:00 A.M., so I could stay with William right up till Monday morning. "Our love affair is not very sensible geographically," he used to say, and he would try to make my departures as easy as possible. Besides, he always loved getting up early.

One poem of his from that period shows the full range of his love for the "sweet Thames," which flows through his life and work:

WINTER ON THE RIVER

dawn

A long orange knife slits the darkness
from ear to ear. Flat sheets of Kansas
have been dropped where the water was.
A blue snake is lying perfectly still,
freezing to avoid detection—no, it is the barge-road.

noon

It's six weeks past the solstice. What
is the sun thinking of? It skulks
above the southern woods at noon.
                              Two ducks descend
on the thin creek that snakes through the plain of ice.
They dream of a great flood coming
to devastate this plastic geography.
We can all remember other things than snow.

dusk

At dusk the east bank glows a colder orange,
giving back heat reluctantly. (The sickle moon
gives it back quickly.) The snake is glacier-green

where an oil-barge has lately churned it.
Tonight unlucky creatures will die, like so many
soldiers or parents, it is nobody's fault.

midnight

The farm dogs bark at a soft crash far up-river:
the ice-breaker is coming down. We go out
in the clear night to see the lights—beacons
on the river, pharos in the sky, and a jewelled
seafarer bringing water to the parched plain.
The hollow roar grows slower than an avalanche.
Her search-light feeling a way from point
of land to point of land, she pulls herself along
by beacon-roots. For a half-mile reach of river
she sights on us, a group of goblins blinking
in front of their white house. Sugary rime
feathers from the bow. An emerald and a garnet
flank the twitching eye.
                            Abruptly she turns,
offering the beam of a ship that has nothing to do with us.
A houseful of strangers passes, ship-noise thumping.

Down-river, other dogs take up the work.
They are clearing a path for the barges of cold
and silence which the creatures are expecting.

Those prophetic dogs. I wonder at William's work sometimes.
Sometimes it is as though he predicted the barges of cold and
silence that have come to fill his life. Can I come to accept that
"it is nobody's fault"? The ironies have become so routine. Now
I am the first one up in the morning, trying to make things easier
for him, writing poems to remember and preserve our love.

WINTER LESSON

There were nights the snow began as powder
dusting the ceramic bulldog on the step
until by morning he wore a white bowler
or was buried altogether. Others,

these gentle fields became moonscape,
a polished crust thick enough to
hold a man without snowshoes. Clear then,
with brittle stars and a freeze so deep
the earth seemed finally irreparable—
you would die if you went too far from home.

Often I lay like a spoiled hibernating bear
after too many nightcaps or excesses
sure the cold would numb me to death, when
the cave grew warmer somehow with dreams of
plump fish hiding in the rainbows of spring streams.

Once I actually woke and stumbled down to
catch you in your father's woolen bathrobe
feeding logs into the wood stove, a dream too.

Twice a night throughout winter and just before
dawn smashed through the kitchen and required
breakfast, you danced this ritual. Sometimes I came down
to smoked ham and eggs over light and remembered to
complain how cold I'd been and how your odd movements
wakened me in the night. The heat I accepted like air.

Now I sit in the same woolen robe
wondering how soon the light will come, and
if these logs will hold till then. You
can't take the stairs as well anymore. Your
circulation's poor. Sometimes you shake a little
in your sleep. I hold you tighter till it's over
or I stoke the fire. I know the ritual like a
well-trained dancing bear. More than habit though,
sometimes the tenderness I come to as I watch you
curl into the warmth of your sleep feels like perfect
instinct, like slapping the wet air to hook a rainbow.

I still find it mysterious how he wakes with a smile when I
shake him out of his sleep to begin the day. This morning he
woke like a baby bird, yawning wide before the eyes even
opened, and then he was up and puttering around trying to help
me get to the race on time. He put off taking a shower and

packed a little overnight bag for his visit with Svetlana. William would visit with this old friend while I finished the race and later went down to New York for the longer run tomorrow. Svetlana was out shopping already when I arrived to drop him off, so I put his suitcase in the little ironing room she had converted into his bedroom on the ground floor so he wouldn't have to use the stairs. He wished me a good run before I tucked him back into bed.

When I finally got to the starting area I searched out the registration tables and picked up my registration bag. Inside I found a bib number, commemorative hat, tube of Ben Gay, and pack of Gator Aid chewing gum. Forty young marines had volunteered to help organize the day. They were lean, beautiful, and very polite but looked on the runners making valiant efforts to warm up as though they were a different species. Every now and then their leader barked out a command and they dropped for a hundred push-ups as effortlessly as they would clip their fingernails. I couldn't resist talking to one of them—blond-haired, with cheeks so rosy they could have been painted on— and asking the name of their mascot.

"Davey, sir!" he shot out, eyes straight ahead.

Davey was an English bulldog dressed in studded collar and regulation camouflage-colored raincoat. I reached down to pet him. My hand sank into a pile of skin and wrinkles. He panted approval.

The race was billed to start at 10:00 sharp, and about that time runners instinctively began to amble up to the starting line. The starting pistol wouldn't fire, so the starter shouted a rather anticlimactic, "Go!" We were off, a formation of marines bringing up the rear as honor guard, singing songs in praise of being a marine as they ran. They chugged along in drill formation as though the heavy black combat boots they wore weighed nothing at all.

About half the runners shot ahead, but I wasn't at all tempted to try to catch them. Tomorrow would be my real test. This morning I was just out for the fun of it.

Sure enough, I found myself running with the sense of elation

Betty had described when participating in an organized race. Hard-working Boy Scouts offered water and orange slices every mile or so, pedestrians clapped us on our way. After the light-house the wind picked up fiercely, but it was at our backs now and the rain had held off. Occasionally, a runner passed me and said hi, but I was enjoying the scenery as much as anything. How much you *see* when you run streets you've only driven before, the grand old summer mansions lined up along the riverbank, sailboats scudding along the water, the ferry to Orient Point making its proud way across the sound, which always reminds me of William's carrier poem. He doesn't give much credit to the juvenilia written those years he served as a pilot in World War II and Korea, but I go back to the poems like a kid who can't get enough stories about what *his* dad was up to "during the war."

CARRIER

She troubles the waters, and they part and close
   Like a people tired of an old queen
Who has made too many progresses; and so she goes
Leisurely swift her passage between green
   South islands; careful and helpless through the locks;
At lazy anchor huge and peacock vain.
On the streaked sea at dawn she stands to the streaks
   And when her way and the wind have made her long,
The planes rise heavy from her whining deck.
Then the bomb's luck, the gun's poise and chattering,
   The far-off dying, are her near affair;
With her sprung creatures become weak or strong
   She watches them down the sky and disappear,
   Heart gone, sea-bound, committed all to air.

In what seemed like no time at all I came running through the chute to the finish line. One of the officials asked for my num-ber, which he couldn't see. He instructed me in a stern tone always to wear my bib number on the *front* of my shirt. Then suddenly, over the PA system, he boomed out: "Dick Harteis just coming in now, ladies and gentlemen. Let's give him a hand." It was such a shock I almost flew into the hot dog stand.

As soon as we had come to a stop at the end of the chute, a volunteer handed us a slip of paper to fill in our name and address. I handed the slip over to a sailor all buttoned up in tight pants and bib shirt, straddling two chairs while he registered our numbers on a big board. He put it in a pile of numbers to be registered before I realized that the slip indicated how I had finished in the race.

I stood around eating pieces of orange, watching him work. But I was getting very stiff, and rather than waiting for my number to go up, I decided I'd better go meet William at Svetlana's. There was bound to be a good lunch ready.

This dear old friend will soon be ninety and still keeps her house with the same largesse that greeted guests when her grandfather was commander of the fortress at St. Petersburg. Years before Stalin's daughter made the name famous, the Russian Orthodox synod had given permission for her to be named for her godfather's battleship, since he was an officer in the Russian navy. She fled the revolution with very little, and later when she escaped World War II Europe all she gained for her trouble was a spaniel left in her care by the grand duke Dmitri. Hers has been a long life of ministering to other people's children, dogs, and guests ever since, even though she still teaches college Russian to put the best vodka on the table.

Her house itself is a ramshackle affair with an enormous porch hidden under ancient pine trees that keep it cool on the hottest days. In the summer you might easily be visiting a rundown mansion out of Chekhov, or a New England inn that has fallen on hard times. The table is always brimming, however. Frozen Stolichnaya, thick as oil, fuels conversation. The parade of guests and relatives coming through from July 4 through Labor Day would fill a number of Tolstoy novels. She is something like a one-woman Statue of Liberty, welcoming refugees from various wars and the hectic pace of American life. One of my favorite habitués is Iryna.

They called her "the ginger girl" in the war, and she spent two years in a Polish concentration camp when the Germans discovered she was working for the Resistance army and helping English prisoners of war. She never got the Order of the Garter, but she wrote successfully enough after the war to make her way to America with an infant son. Things didn't work out well here, though, and after some years of teaching she makes her way as best she can with odd jobs. Her hair is still a luxurious red-gold in color. She takes an interest in what I'm doing, and appreciates my life with William.

"Richard, run good," she said in her thick Polish accent when I saw her last, "so we can all be proud of you."

Stayed in bed till one o'clock. Wonderful luxury after rising early yesterday morning for the big run. Yesterday my bladder got me out of bed, this morning the urge to rub down with Ben Gay.

One can understand taking a number of nervous pees the morning before a twenty-five-kilometer run. This was only to be a trial run to see if I could begin to approach the longer distances of a marathon. My training wasn't really on the line yet. But I kept going to the bathroom so often yesterday morning, I thought it would be a week before such a need would arise again. Wonderful to be so empty, yet full of nervous energy.

The longer runs are to act as little rehearsals for the marathon in all details, so last night I gave up my diet and dutifully overloaded on the carbohydrates recommended as the best fuel for the day of the run. "Last supper" pasta parties are standard fare before long races, but I added a hot fudge sundae for good measure. Can't be too careful. The morning of the race, however, the diet is more spartan: a little toast, coffee maybe, if you normally have it, and some juice if the acid doesn't bother you.

I carefully wrapped a twenty-dollar bill and the apartment keys in a plastic baggie and tucked them into the little pocket in my jogging shorts. I also included the name and phone number of the friend with whom I was staying should something happen to me during the run. Poor Jim Fixx, a relatively young man, the high guru of marathon running, died of a heart attack some years ago while training. Well-meaning friends always point this tragedy out to you, as well as the recent opinion that sports walking is as good as or better than jogging. But who knows? Maybe all those years of exercise kept Jim Fixx alive well beyond the years his medical condition might normally have afforded him.

The weather forecast called for rain, but I decided that after a few miles I would be plenty warm and the rain would be more refreshing than annoying. For insurance I took along a thin running jacket that I could tie around my waist and have available for the finish if need be.

When my taxi pulled up to the West Side YMCA, runners were streaming in from all directions dressed in various outfits, from plastic bags to nylon shorts as brief as bikinis. They were everywhere, bending and stretching, changing clothes, chatting nervously about the hills up on 110th Street, or bragging about the number of miles they were running each week. The scene had the feeling of a country fair or a medieval jousting event. There were even red, white, and blue banners flying in the breeze proclaiming the New York Road Runners Club Twenty-five-Kilometer Tune-Up. I got my free T-shirt and official number at registration in the little theater: Richard Harteis M41 Tune-Up Number 1565. Forty-one-year-old male—why do they have to publicize your age every time you enter a race? Not forty, forty-one. Incredible. Once I overheard one of William's friends from the old days complain that she was about to have her seventy-second birthday. She said she just couldn't *believe* she had reached that age. Would I ever have thought in high school, say, or college that one day I would be an M41 hoping to be able to make it through a 15.5-mile run?

Surprisingly, the only description of the course to be run was a hand-drawn sketch someone had tacked up on the door. Presumably, it was all well marked or everyone running was a New Yorker. I studied it for a while and copied it down just in case:

The first loop would take us up to 102nd Street and back to our starting point. The second loop would go to 110th Street and back again to the starting point, and a third time we would head up to 110th Street, back to 59th at the head of the park, then finish at Tavern on the Green, a fancy restaurant set just inside Central Park. Brunch was already being served there under trees strung with thousands of little white twinkle lights. A strolling accordion player played French café tunes.

On the day of a race it is very easy to strike up conversations with people. There is a lovely vulnerability about runners standing around dressed in next to nothing who are about to begin

NYC MARATHON TUNE-UP
Richard Harteis–M41   NYRRC# .....

1565

🍎 **New York Road Runners Club**

something rather difficult, nothing to identify them—a business suit, a surgeon's gown, a cop uniform—in the roles they normally play. It is a little like the democratization of military service or a patient's feeling of being stripped to the core of personality as he is wheeled naked into the operating room.

Anything dealing with the state of your bowels, your feet, your knees, or your training is a suitable topic for discussion. People tend to prefer the anonymity of first names only, however, and if there is any place you do not ask a person's occupation or marital status, it's at a race.

Such caution is far from antisocial, though. Runners have come for one thing only, the race. And they are likely to speak with you more intimately about their apprehensions, their joy, their problems, than they might even to a spouse or confessor—certainly more than they would to a common stranger. They have come to compete against the clock and their own notion of what their limits are. So the race is not really a question of competition among runners. There's actually an *esprit de corps* that one usually finds in team sports.

A nice guy named Brad, about my age and build but slightly balding, walked me over to the carousel in the park where we were to start. A little old woman was in charge of the roped-off area that served as the baggage claim. Most of the runners carried only a gym bag of no great value, but it was clever to have an elderly volunteer act as honor guard. Since any thief worth his salt could easily have made off with half the bags anyway, a little old lady for security guard was probably the most effective system they could have set up.

Brad took Vaseline out of his gym bag and offered me the jar. We went through the ritual of greasing up and began some warm-up and stretching exercises. Over the next half hour more and more people began to show up at the starting area, and the lines at the portable johns began to lengthen.

A little lost, runners milled about until officials strung up a big starting banner over the road. Light rock and roll played on the PA system to calm everyone down. Posters with the numbers 5,6,7, and 8 went up on high poles to mark the minutes per mile runners hoped to maintain during the race. If you knew you only ran a ten-minute mile, it made no sense to go to the head of the line where you would only get in the way of faster runners and maybe get trampled in the process. There were plenty of miles to catch up if you planned to put on a big push. All very civilized. I had no idea how I'd do, so I went to the back of the crowd where they didn't even bother to post a running time.

Grete Waitz, women's winner of a number of marathons, came to the microphone on crutches. An injury would keep her from competing this year, but she would do the honors of starting the runners off in this Tune-Up. Five, four, three. She wished us all luck in her singsong Scandinavian and promised to return to the race again next year. I had trouble seeing her and bobbed up and down like the other runners to catch a glimpse. Then, slowly, as in a dream, without any particular event to trigger it that I could see, the line began to thin out up ahead.

We were off. Several thousand men and women of every age began jogging slowly through the park, chatting amiably, waiting to see how the day would go.

For the first five miles or so the pack hung fairly close together, as though it felt a strength in numbers and feared strik-
ing out individually, a kind of atavistic self-preservation. The
stray gazelle separated from the herd falls prey to the lion or wild
dogs.

Most of the runners were by no means professional athletes,
but anyone who had entered the race had been training and
could easily run five miles without too much difficulty. Gradually, though, the runners began to wilt a little, the pack thinned
out, and conversation became sporadic interjections about the
course. "What time?" "Water there." "All right."

People began to enter the private twilight zone reserved for
each runner's imagination. Would it be too farfetched to compare this stage to the lonely process of dying? Each runner was
dealing with his unique aches and pains in his own particular
way, each kept his own counsel and made his best judgment on
how to keep doing the difficult work, each slipped into private
meditations on the person in front of him. Would it rain, why
had he treated his brother so badly last time he visited, how did
the blue and green colors in the Perrier running shorts blend
into the color of the Mediterranean Sea, what mile was he coming to, would he make it to the end of the race? Even the exhila-
ration and adrenalin that were fueling this effort were a little like
the light or grace we are told is sent sometimes to meet the
challenge of dying.

Occasionally people would drop off the track to relieve themselves in the woods or behind a convenient building. Last week
we had supper with William's ninety-two-year-old stepmother,
and she found this the most interesting aspect of my running
project: how one could run that far without taking a pee, or what
one did about it exactly. The actual running of the race she
seemed to find less impressive.

There were as many different gaits as there were runners.
Some had a little fanny-shaking style, like duck waddling. Some
threw their legs out from the knees only and kept their torso
motionless as a belly dancer or native woman bearing a jug of
water on her head. There were even a few who hobbled along

with a plastic leg but managed to keep a rhythm that resembled running. Occasionally someone would come loping through like a white-tailed deer, while others rolled along like tortoises in their wheelchairs. Maybe half of the runners wore some sort of ankle or knee support.

At the end of the first hour or so the park began to fill up with New Yorkers taking their pleasure on a Sunday morning. Indignant matrons in mink stood waiting for a break in the runners so they could cross the road. Intense bag ladies took inventory of their possessions. The homeless lay stretched out on park benches or under trees. Affluent young couples on ten-speeds, gay guys on roller skates, babies in buggies, and teenagers on skateboards took advantage of the park roads, which had been closed off to traffic.

When you came to a little group of fans who applauded you on, your pace picked up as surely as a laboratory mouse running on a treadmill, laying it on for a piece of cheddar. It took some effort not to blush or smile too broadly. Water stations every couple of miles became more and more refreshing, proving once again how important it is to keep hydrated. I will pray every night that we aren't going through an Indian summer on November 1. I believe one year a runner actually did collapse and die during a particularly hot marathon.

At about mile eight I noticed that I'd been running beside a cute little guy wearing earphones and a green T-shirt like mine.

"Hi, how you doing?" I said in standard greeting.

"Great."

His name was David, from Manhattan, could have been a stockbroker, a waiter, anything.

"I forgot my earphones today, darn it. You like running with them?"

"Yeah, it helps pass the time. Sometimes I listen to a ball game, you know. Wanta try?"

"No, that's okay, thanks. How fast do you think we're going?"

"Ten-minute miles, no more. I like to start off kind of slow."

"Well, this is as fast as I plan to go. I just want to make it to the finish line."

"You'll make it."

We ran together in silence but felt each other's welcome company for a few miles until I taught myself a very important lesson.

"Hey, David," I said in what was meant to be a humorous tone. "What do you say we stop and have a nice cold beer?"

He didn't say a word, but gradually picked up his speed and drifted ahead into the crowd. I realized immediately that he was having just as hard a time as anyone else and that he couldn't afford a single negative thought if he was going to finish, even something that might try to pass as a joke. I never saw him again.

Oh, well, guess I'll go eat worms. Wherever you are, David, I'm sorry. But as I say, it was a lesson, and this *is* what sports is about in part. Just like life. Make your mistakes, learn some sportsmanship, and keep on trucking.

At the end of the second loop it turned out that the hills everyone was worrying about during the warm-up for the race were only long inclines in the landscape compared with Ryan's Hill, which I'd been running at home. I kept waiting for the killer to materialize, and when I asked the person next to me, "When are we coming to the hill?" she laughed as though I had made a somewhat funny joke. It turned out that we were already on our way down.

At some point as we came close to the starting line again and had run just a little better than half the course, the PA system jolted us out of our concentration. "Make room for the lead runner, make room for the lead runner." Incredibly, some character had already finished the third lap and was coming home to the finish line. From behind me I could hear runners applaud as he ran by, and then he was passing me too, on his toes, trim as a jockey, blond hair thinning a little, every muscle in his shoulders and legs visible as an anatomy lesson. He wouldn't have been my idea of "Mr. Right" if we had met on the beach somewhere, but this guy was born to run, beautiful as a yearling filly gamboling across some spring green.

"Go man," I called out after him. "Go."

I don't know why it was, really, perhaps that I was watching something wonderful and I knew from inside just how wonderful, but I had to wipe away tears as I watched him disappear toward the finish line.

When I reached the top of the hill a second time I knew I would make it. I still had at least four miles to go, and earlier I had taught myself another lesson for which I was paying the price. When you are in a rhythm and have pushed the joints and ligaments to the maximum, you have to be very careful of the least little awkward stress that breaks that pattern. Several miles before, I had reached down to scratch my calf when an insect bit me, throwing the whole of my weight out of line as I ran. It was as though I had inadvertently landed in a manhole. My left ankle was burning, and I felt as though someone had taken a club to my lower back. I knew I could take the pain till the finish, but I was afraid I might do enough damage to keep me from continuing my training for the marathon. "Running through" an injury was forbidden by all the manuals despite what any high school coach ever said to an athlete in pain. Running with a torn muscle or ligament only made the matter severely worse in the acute phase.

On the other hand, could I be playing tricks on myself? Was I really just too tired to continue and looking for an excuse to stop at a respectable point in the race? I wasn't winded, and aside from the ankle, there was no particular pain. I was pretty sure I hadn't broken anything. I did, however, certainly understand by now what was meant by the "natural erosion of the body's resources." I could conceivably explain to everyone that I really could have finished but thought it better for my training to stop, to respect one's injury and all that. But I knew how wormy I'd feel if I had to go through that song and dance.

I decided to push on and limp to save the ankle as best I could. It wasn't so much a conscious decision to go on as it was a decision not to think about it anymore, to let time take care of the problem. "In one hour I will have finished this race. I will watch time pass. I will think of time and discount what my body is going through until the time has passed."

At mile eleven or twelve you are in something like that semiconscious state just before you really decide to get out of bed in the morning. The thoughts are all occurring, but you aren't aware that *you* are thinking those thoughts. It's a little like the sensation our friend Blanche was describing to us recently. She came for lunch last week, and we finally wound up agreeing that her obsession with meditation was not unlike the obsession a runner suffers. Over the cream of mussel soup she described how that morning she had become a green frog at the feet of the yogi, telling her whole life in ambiguous little "ribbets," and then how a golden light took her over and she flew to a black sun that turned out to be an eye through which she flew, and how it became clear that the rushing in and out of the stars she breathed was just like God breathing in and out to create the universe.

The Southern lady who had wanted to meet Blanche and joined us for lunch kept saying how *interesting* this all was since she had absolutely *no* imagination herself and was sure she could never have such visions. The only problem was that Blanche didn't exactly consider them "just" visions. What I thought was legitimate skepticism Blanche considered unenlightened cynicism.

"Well, what's reality anyway?" I said, when I saw that I was beginning to offend. "Even science is just a way of looking at things. We change the rules of reality every time a new Einstein turns up, don't we? I just see it in simple psychological terms, like being able to tap into the dream center in your brain, or whatever, to resolve conflict. But maybe I'm just wearing Freudian blinders. Maybe there is some sort of reality behind what you are seeing in meditation."

I denied ever feeling an endorphin "high" from running, but I did have to admit that running every day produced a psychological sense of well-being, a kind of tingling throughout the day that was sorely missed if I was unable to run on a given day. And yes, occasionally I seemed to be able to manipulate time for my own purposes as I ran, and sometimes running took on a moral dimension, maybe, where I could see my effort as a kind of prayer in the physical world that touched another realm.

What right did I have to patronize Blanche? She had certainly shown strength in the challenges life had thrown her, worked hard to become a successful novelist, achieved peace with herself and her family and her lover. What right had I to put down her exotic attempts to grow in spirit? She was already a hell of a lot more generous with people than I would ever be, had gone a little farther down the pilgrim's road.

"You see, Richard," she said with one of the sweetest smiles ever to come out of South Carolina, "your running is a kind of meditation too."

As I came limping into the last mile of the race, I had started giving out little grunts as I ran. I wasn't out of breath, but making some noise seemed to help move me physically toward the finish line. There were all sorts of runners who came in after me—young and old, men and women—but as I came within view of the finish I found myself running beside a black woman in her fifties dressed in red shorts, singlet, and sweatband over her short graying Afro. Her head was bowed and her thick legs were barely moving. Young black women along the finish line recognized her and shouted her on.

"How you doing?" I asked.

She looked at me sideways like a beaten dog, then flashed a full smile as bright as the sun coming through the clouds.

"You and me are going to *make* it," she said.

I could see the clock over the finish line read two hours forty minutes and forty seconds. I began sprinting to see if I could cross before the minute was out. I didn't. My time came in at two hours forty-one minutes and five seconds. But I made it, all right. I made it.

Dear Betty,

When are you coming home? We miss you. Please plan a visit (or two!) soon. October 13 we go to Phoenix to the Udalls', then on for a medical conference and visit with my sister in San Diego till the nineteenth. Otherwise, we'll be here like sitting ducks. We found two trees that would be perfect for your new deck, but you have to come collect them.

I did the Tune-Up Race you suggested in two hours and forty minutes. Not a great time, but a *great time,* as you suggested. I'm sending my ID tags along as proof.

At dinner last night our hostess—my age, very pretty—kept grilling me about what pleasure I could possibly find in training for a marathon. How could I explain the excitement of running with all those folks? I even sprinted over the finish line. That turned out to be a dumb thing to do, I now discover. Probably the worst time to pour it on is after you've stretched those tendons to the limit. My left ankle is still very sore. I broke it in three places once when I was skiing. I was coming down a glacier in Switzerland and got going so fast I went catatonic in a tuck until my ski caught on something and I self-destructed. Until now, though, it hasn't bothered me. I hope to baby it enough to start with you November 1, never fear.

We got a call yesterday informing us that William's *Partial Accounts* has won this year's *Los Angeles Times* Book Award. Ironic, since we've joined with poets around the country protesting their decision to discontinue poetry reviews. But nothing would be gained by refusing the honor. They said that if William couldn't come they'd like me to come out for him, and if not they would send a film crew to tape his acceptance. We've decided to go and see if we can't be a Trojan horse (Trojan Pegasus?), lobbying for the cause during the festivities there.

I'm so happy for William. It's such a beautiful book, and

finally people are beginning to give it the attention it deserves. Is there any chance you'll be visiting Penn at that time and could join us?

Paul and Kitty Townsend want to come to New York for the marathon. They can watch the race with William on TV and act as our body baggers if we don't make it. Could you put up their son Robert if he comes along?

Give us a call. We really have missed you. Much love from

R and W

October 3 — Yom Kippur

Gray skies, chilly weather. All weekend cantors have been wailing repentance and extolling God's beauty on public radio programs. This morning as I ran I had to face the fact that I might not make this marathon run after all, a thought that has depressed me these past few days.

A week ago one of William's former students came with her intense husband for a visit. Very sweet folks, a poet and a painter. Shy, poor, not very at home in the world, but deeply in love with each other and with a feeling for William bordering on reverence. I left them for my long Sunday run, sure they would be content to have William walk the grounds and point out all the exotic trees he planted years ago when he ran a little nursery as a hobby. Japanese maple, pin oak, Chinese elm, weeping hemlock, and dogwood stand next to one another in democratic abandon. When William finally gave up the hobby the stock was too big to move, and the tree-lined walkways down to the formal garden and river grew up like some bizarre American version of Versailles.

Before I began training sometimes I would see some beautiful young man or woman running out on the open highway toward the college. It was clear they were long-distance runners, and it seemed so neat that they could just take off and run to the next town, say, ten miles up the road. Last Sunday I decided to get off the treadmill and fulfill my fantasy of running to the college and back. My ankle still gave me trouble, but according to *The Injured Runner's Handbook,* I was only experiencing second-degree pain: "The pain remains constant or increases slightly as your runs continue, and may remain for a few hours after. It has little effect on your running form."

The day was perfect autumn, leaves just beginning to change, even a little too cool. When I turned off the loop I normally make and up the hill to the main route running through the little villages on its way to the college, it was like cutting classes, or telling the boss to shove it. And who would have ever believed the main highway would be so interesting? I'd gotten used to every dog, every house, every fancy tree on my loop, but the highway was like another country. Nathan's Country Store had planted a hedge of yellow corn and large red dahlias around the parking lot. How had I missed that in the thousands of trips I'd taken to the college? There was a new Chinese restaurant in the little shopping mall. Ted Johnson kept his lobster pots stored behind his garage where anyone could just pop down and pick up a few. These were no earthshaking discoveries, one might say, but they were diverting enough that I hardly minded the seven-mile run to the college.

On the way back, before I turned onto the country road to our house, I stopped to pick some milkweed plants whose pods were erupting along the highway in spectacular cornucopia fashion. I thought I'd carry them back to David to sketch, since he'd missed a session with a live model by staying with William for me while I ran. When I started running again, my ankle felt like shattered glass, and a burning pain flamed up the Achilles tendon to the calf. Foolishly, I limped on home still running. And, instead of warming down and treating the leg, I helped our guest take care of a flat tire he had discovered as he was packing the car.

Monday morning, my off day, I was as stiff and sore as I thought I'd be. I walked around in the manner of a robot. By Tuesday it was clear that I'd advanced to third-degree pain: "You feel mild pain on easy runs, which gets worse as the runs progress, and severe pain on hard runs. The pain definitely interferes with proper running form. It continues after your run and usually is present throughout the day."

That was me, all right. I simply was unable to stop limping as I ran, and my calf knotted before I even got to Ryan's Hill. I walked home and consulted the instructions for third-degree pain:

> Start very slowly and cautiously after at least 10 minutes of brisk walking. When the pain builds up to a form-disturbing level, walk and do some easy stretching exercises for the muscle groups around

the injured area. Note: If the muscle or tendon is inflamed, stretching it will delay the healing process. Alternate running and walking
according to how you feel. The object is to keep moving and stay
within the limits of safe running that your pain will set for you. At
this level, you may be better off to stop running and switch to an
aerobic alternative until you can run at least at the second-degree
level of pain.

Better off to stop running! In exactly one month I am supposed to run 26.2 miles, and these next weeks are to be the peak
of my training if I hope to finish. All of my hard work will be
ruined. How can I possibly not run the marathon this year?

I began poring over the text for some advice that might give
me hope, and it was like finding the Rosetta Stone when I came
across such advice in the chapter entitled "Running Through an
Injury": "Forcing yourself to continue to train may make things
worse. Often a day or two off will allow you to return sooner to
quality training than if you had continued to aggravate your
injury. Total rest beyond two or three days will not help many
injuries. You may as well continue to run, or take up an alternative exercise, but within certain limits."

Well, that was it, I decided. Things weren't so bad. I wouldn't
lose my conditioning if I took two days off, and meanwhile I
would start rowing a little to keep my wind up. Whew!

A nice woman in the training room at the college, Miss Horn,
took an interest in my problem and let me come in to use the
whirlpool Thursday afternoon. She even gelled me up and ran an
ultrasound transducer over the ankle to help speed healing. The
sound waves massage deeper and clear away breakdown products
in a way that the whirlpool doesn't, she explained. And mercifully, the very next day I felt a lot better, though the ankle
remained a problem. One more day, I decided, and I'd be back
at level two of pain and able to run again. Betty would be proud
of me for using my *resources* properly.

Friday morning I called up Billy Bettmann and invited him to
lunch. His mother was one of William's favorite students, and
when his parents brought him to start his freshman year she

stopped by the house to ask us to keep an eye on him. We had been meaning to call him, and when we did I was doubly glad to find that he had gone out for crew. He might give me a few pointers on rowing until I could return to running.

What a sweet kid he is, lanky, a little shy, dressed down in old jeans and a T-shirt in the current fashion. He devoured everything put in front of him, which was gratifying, and after diet pistachio pudding we all started down to the river. There were plenty of carcasses, and the dead fish smell still permeated the humid air. I rowed us out to the middle of the river, and after giving me a few instructions on the proper use of oar and how to get the most out of my effort, Billy promptly fell asleep in the bow. He had pulled his first all-nighter preparing for a mid-term exam, and the gentle swells rocking the dory were too much for him. William sat in silence like an old sea captain on the lookout for a nor'easter. The wind caught Mikey's ears and turned them into little sails. Occasionally, he turned his nose up on the air to smell out some neighbor dog. I was careful not to get too close to three wild swans paddling out of our way toward the shore. Lately Mikey's taken to chasing the swans for diversion, then coming back to shake himself out all over the guests and trying to milk a little appreciation. Sometimes, though, the swans hold their ground and snap at him ferociously enough to pluck off his nose neat as an olive.

He's getting a little too country, this dog, comes in to eat then is gone all day running with the other dogs on the place or shaking out the rug of cats spread in front of the door down at the Dawleys' house. He's gotten lean and smells a little too much like fish. He's got ring around the collar, and we don't let him sleep on the bed these days. Sometimes he runs halfway to New London and we get a call from our neighbor Roger to come fetch him.

They say dogs can't live without people, that when they agreed to become domesticated they had to find something to replace the social comfort of the pack. But Mickey's been disproving that theory of late. Sometimes I take him along when I run and play out my surrogate role to the letter. He goes crazy

with pleasure when he sees me with his leash. But my doctor says
it isn't good for dogs to go jogging with you. Something about
their brain sloshing around and banging against the skull so hard
they sometimes give themselves a concussion. Seems a little farfetched to me. I can't imagine a dog blacking out as it tries to
run down a stag, for example, but Mikey has joint problems too,
and I don't want to provoke his old injury.

Once after we came back to D.C. from a vacation I forgot to

(c) Mimi Levine, 1988.

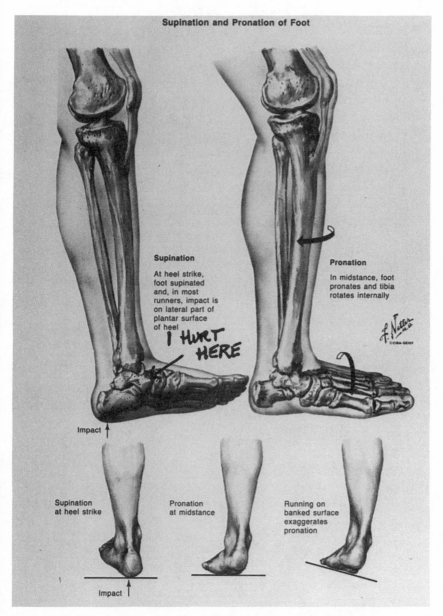

Supination and Pronation of Foot

Supination

At heel strike, foot supinated and, in most runners, impact is on lateral part of plantar surface of heel

I HURT HERE

Pronation

In midstance, foot pronates and tibia rotates internally

Impact ↑

Supination at heel strike

Pronation at midstance

Running on banked surface exaggerates pronation

Impact ↑

lock the front gate. I heard a car screech, a bang-bang, and when I went out William stood catatonic at the bottom of the drive listening to Mikey cry beneath the motorist's car. Poor Mikey was tangled up in the transmission; when he stopped crying I figured that was *it* for him, and went across the street to take William away. But Mikey disengaged himself somehow and came limping across the street, filthy as a garage mechanic, his pupils like large black saucers from the shock. They wired his knee joint in a figure eight, and the scar formation served as a replacement tendon. I think he's a little blind in the one eye, but so far the miracle tendon is doing just fine. The offending joint

Credit: *Thomas W. Cline, Princeton University.*

in both our cases is pictured above. As a point of reference and by way of coincidence I also include a photo of normal (A and B) and abnormal (C and D) fruit fly forelegs that appeared in William's *Princeton Alumni Weekly* for September 30. Such intellectual ferment at Princeton these days!

Mikey seems to have healed up just fine, and in spite of what Dr. Brensilver says I still occasionally take him along on the shorter runs. Use it or lose it, they say.

I'm feeling a little desperate about my own healing process, though. I've taken two days off. I even paid eighty-four dollars for a new pair of Tiger Gels, a running shoe with packets of gel built-in to the heel and toe for cushioning and extra support. But my ankle still won't give me more than three miles without the burning pain. A week's rest is the most I can afford without losing my conditioning, according to the manuals. If anything, I'm supposed to be at my maximum training now.

Yom Kippur. Gray skies. Chilly weather. I'm as frustrated as a child being kept indoors with a cold. Just last week Mikey and I were out doing road work, not a cloud in the sky, laying it on as we came down Ryan's Hill past Roger's house. Now I'm stuck in my studio ruminating on my bad luck, hoping it will all work out. What a fragile work is man. I already miss my runs, but I guess I have no choice but to rest the ankle some more. I feel as helpless as the orange kitten that the goddamn crows flew away with last week, and I can't seem to get that bad omen out of my mind's eye.

THE CROWS

Rather blond or fawn or wheat field
my yellow lab, my chunky Mikey
sailing over piles of leaves,
a golden cloud trailing baggy me
to the British neighbor, Roger, and midnight
dark or ink of the squid but certainly
more than crow black crows lounging
on his Monday morning garbage cans

with their six tiny eyes, dull as death
to stop us shorter than a Plexiglas wall.

Myopic Mikey snorts and prances,
barks after a little reassurance—
Roger gave up on Mikey's IQ when
he couldn't learn to lie on his back
and "die for the Queen."—Then again,
Roger leaves his Christmas lights up
year round which the neighbors
prefer to find slightly eccentric
rather than slothful or stupid.

The crows hop lethargically
like their ugly vulture cousins
and roost with their prey—
a tiny orange kitten—
on a string of lights
below the Star of Bethlehem
in Roger's blue spruce.

Our stride broken, the morning air
is rancid suddenly with rotting
fish and garbage. I'm getting
cold and stiff. Instinct tells me
to pick up a rock and throw it at
the dark creatures staining the trees
when lovely Roger, waving from
his kitchen window, flashes the
Christmas lights on and off fast,
and the crows lumber off
for another day.

Full moon, autumn equinox, even a lunar eclipse predicted. If there was ever a time to begin again, tonight is the night. The model here at William's sculpture class has even gone faint. Everyone is congregated around the coffee pot while she pulls herself together. "Syncope of unknown etiology"—very hard to find out why someone's gone faint. Are you diabetic, have you been ill lately, has this ever happened before? Pulse a little thin, but regular. The old obsession, the queasy stomach when emergencies arise, and you're the only one with medical training.

In the beginning I used to turn around on the highway for every parked car to make sure no one lay slumped across the front seat with a heart attack. The old terror of responsibility. Make it stop hurting, will I get better, what do you think it is, Doc? On a train or a plane, "Is there a doctor on board? Please come to the front if there is a doctor." And your heart sinks as you get out of your seat. What will it be awaiting you?

You do the best you can, try not to project nervousness, seek help when something has you baffled. And you never treat your own family, the cardinal rule. It's hard enough when the patient is virtually unknown to you, but impossible to be objective with people you love, or cause the pain that is sometimes necessary when you're treating a patient.

In my years in medicine the heart attacks, the massive trauma of car crashes, even the burn cases will never overshadow a simple little problem I encountered when I was starting.

I was alone at the office in Rabat when a crusty old field engineer came in from Casablanca complaining that his hearing was shot. In five minutes, to his relief and amazement, I had solved the problem by taking a wire loop and carefully working out a plug of earwax. A moment later he wiped his jaw and said, "What's this?" When he saw that it was blood pouring from his ear, he went gray and an ashen horror clouded his features, a look that said, "What in God's name have you *done* to me?"

I tried looking into his ear with the otoscope, but it was like descending through the atmosphere of Mars. I couldn't see where the bleeding was coming from, and I couldn't get it to stop. I was so scared I finally had to leave the room for a minute, and until the day I die I will thank God for the little proof He gave that He listens to prayer and intervenes in the daily lives of men. Dr. Gallopin happened to be coming back from lunch as I came hurrying out of the examining room as though I were Dr. Jekyll trying to fend off Mr. Hyde's onslaught.

"The ear canal is filled with little capillaries," he said. "Just pack it with cotton. It will stop in a minute." He didn't even bother to take a look at the patient, thinking the problem insignificant, or perhaps wanting to help me save face.

Oh, Dr. Gallopin, where are you now? Make it stop hurting. Will I get better? What do you think it is? In exactly twenty-five days I am supposed to run the New York Marathon, and I can't even walk up a flight of stairs right. Two more days of rest have made practically no difference, and in the next two weeks I am scheduled to reach the pinnacle of my training. I've even put on a few extra pounds while I've waited for things to improve. What am I going to do?

If Betty were around she'd have some advice. Instead, today's mail brings a postcard from Mallorca showing a nine-curve switchback in the road up Soller Mountain.

25 September Lluc-Alcari

Dear Friends,

This is the road I am training on, Richard. No wonder I breeze through the marathon! The weather is still gorgeous here, and I'm seeing lots of friends and family. Hope you two will come with me some summer.

Love,
Betty

"No wonder I breeze through the marathon!" Even the stock market has gone to hell today, biggest single drop in history. What is going on here?

The only bright spot lately has been Josephine and Eric's visit, dear old friends, both in their eighties now, migrating south for the winter. This year they have finally sold the house they've gone to in New Hampshire every summer for fifty years, to make it possible to enter a retirement community at some point. Closing out fifty years of life. They've even had to leave the dear ashes of a favorite grandchild scattered among the flowers around the rock consecrated one summer afternoon to serve as a monument. How can they come to us so civilized, so selfless, so filled with intelligent good will and acceptance? There has to be some sort of special grace we're given to face the awful challenge of giving up the sweet world.

I got my two cents' worth in last spring when Josephine introduced me at the Library of Congress. The greatest part of that honor, I said, was to be chosen by a poet of such spiritual authority. She is modest, not secretive about her Roman Catholic faith, but would never dream of proselytizing. If you come across just one person in life, though, whose brilliance and intellectual honesty you are absolutely sure of, and that person has attempted a life of faith from her earliest years, she alone can sustain an agnostic's effort to cross over all his life.

I have a recollection of Josephine at the Library of Congress that friends say is too dramatic to be true, but I'll stick by it, at least the informing spirit of the anecdote that proves the point.

On a dais filled with the archangels of the poetry world the only other woman present, a black militant writer, turned up wearing the exact same formal evening dress as Josephine, except that Josephine had added some sort of diamond star-burst brooch to set off the costume. Perhaps it is my catty imagination, but the dress business seemed to infuriate her black doppelgänger. The poems the black writer read were as dark as their black velvet dresses, filled with anger, particularly against patronizing white ladies of the DAR variety. Josephine sat like the Statue of Liberty, her beautiful face floating above her naked shoulders devoid of any emotion except polite attention. Ironically, Josephine's entire career when she was poetry consultant, a job that has since become the Poet Laureateship of the United

States, was an effort to bring black poets to the nation's capital and to reach out to the black community. She felt the generations of suffering racism has produced in our country, knew that the inequities remained great enough to require that black poets give a voice to the rage her colleague was venting.

In William's poem "Revenant" a spirit returns to tell how he frustrated the Roman emperor who had him burned alive. When the victim was placed into the metal sculpture of a bull under which the fires had been laid, he decided he had simply to keep quiet, only thrashing his arms and legs "the way a deaf mute might scream." No sound would bellow out of the sculpture to entertain the guests:

> I gained two stages of progress by that dance
> but Heliogabalus did not profit from my show
> of continence, could not learn anything
> from his iron beast, speaking a blessed silence.
> He was not elevated by that existence.

How often is it better to keep a blessed silence like Josephine on that stage, and how often is it as easy as being burned alive.

Perhaps the only solution to this running problem is to take my cue from souls like Josephine and keep on with the work in silence. And, if I face the humiliation of *walking* the twenty-six miles of the marathon, perhaps I'll just have to accept that the way William accepts the fact that he can't speak easily every morning of his life when he wakes up. I'll make an absolutely rigorous effort to return to a running schedule and start dieting seriously this time. I'll target every day and keep track to see just how far my mentors can take me.

I know it won't be easy, not any easier than the discipline William's had to muster to keep trying, to keep sane even. In another poem, on a night like this, William describes the moon as an angel who teaches him "the real aspect of things." Its light has changed for us now, but still holds the power of instruction:

MOON

Now these dark years later,
it seems the messenger
angel has taken flight.
The moon is just a hole
worked by a pale moth on
the black fabric of night.

She beats her dusty wings
against the sky, hungry
as a lost soul for light.
The dull and powder stars
soil her random wake,
a litany of loss

haphazard as your own
with speech gone and the brain's
lovely light confounded,
the real aspect of things
sure as the reflection
in a funhouse mirror.

When suddenly your gaze
splits the dark like blue light
cracking a block of ice.
You are the lost angel
smiling on the night and
illuminated by

The golden light that pours
through a perfect circle.
"Look," you say, pointing to
the sky, like reaching from
the silver surface of
a mirror, "look, the howl moon."

In the dream I have decided to risk it and let William go off on his own to take care of some small errand. I hear him come in, and when I go to the door I find him apologetic, covered with blood. His two fingers reach up under the skin through a large cut in his forehead, massaging the skull in that area where the third eye is said to reside. We will need to wash out the wound before suturing. I tell him to take his fingers away. There are cuts on his legs and chest. He says he has fallen down, he is sorry. I decide to call an ambulance, he is too bad off for me to drive him to the hospital. An hour later the paramedics arrive. They have walked up the forty flights of stairs to get to us. I ask them why they didn't take the elevator. They tell me they didn't know the building had an elevator.

Mercifully, a bearing goes out in the oil burner, and a racket that sounds like the house is shaking apart wakes me out of the dream. Six o'clock. I turn off the furnace, bring a space heater from the studio to have some warmth in the house when we wake up again, and fish out the maintenance contract with the heating company. Incredibly, someone is manning the twenty-four-hour emergency line and promises a repairman by eleven. In the next three hours the second-shift personnel wake me four times with confirmation calls and calls for directions when the serviceman can't find the house. When he finally arrives at the front door William gets up and spills a full quart of urine from the pee bottle he keeps at the side of the bed during the night. Mikey begins to lap it up with friendly slurps. For some reason, Mrs. Chu arrives early to do speech therapy with William and is knocking on the downstairs door. It is nine-thirty and time to begin my triumphant return to training for the New York City Marathon.

I clean up the mess and send the workman on his way with twice as much money as I think is due—labor is not covered on a zone valve, it turns out, says so right there in small print I mis-took for fly droppings. Since nothing is going quite normally, I sit down with Mrs. Chu and William for a cup of coffee and read a little of what I've been writing. She is happy with it, says it won't matter if I don't finish the marathon, that it's the challenge that matters.

Things have been a little tough for her this past week too. Charles has just retired from a distinguished career as a professor at the college and is settling into his new situation. Her mother has come for a visit and things are delicate. Her mother thinks Charles is a shy Oriental gentleman, since he doesn't say much around her. "But you and I know he isn't shy," Mrs. Chu says.

Once William lent his Vermont house to the Chus and their friends from China, a couple famous around the world for their work as biochemists. Charles and the Chinese husband got so excited when a porcupine started eating the siding off the house, they killed it with a frying pan. Feeling guilty for their enthusiasm, they made the noble, face-saving decision of cooking the spiny rodent for supper.

Mrs. Chu likes the part about Josephine, would like to meet her. I suspect they would get on well.

The first year after *she* retired Mrs. Chu started to go blind, a tumor pushing on the optic nerve. She had it removed last Christmas, and by Easter her sight had completely returned. She believes in miracles. Doesn't think I'll have any problem at all running.

In spite of the fast-moving clouds over the moon, it has not rained this week. Yellow and orange leaves are beginning to cover the road, though, and I make a mental note to be careful of slipping as I begin my run. By the end of the first mile it is clear that I am still going to have trouble. The burning pain surrounds the inner left ankle, and though I could continue, I think my only hope is to start back. As I come to our drive, one of the bees feeding on fallen pears and apples along the road has smacked me right in the forehead, and I want to put a little ammonia on the bite to take the sting out. What a day.

This year the bees have been particularly aggressive, have mated with killers from down south, I think. Mikey dug into a ground nest early in the summer and got himself so stung I thought he'd go into shock. He wouldn't stop hyperventilating even after I fed him Benadryl wrapped in hamburger, and baking soda was applied to the welts that rose on his skin. A luncheon guest came running over and just had to see what was going on as I brushed the bees from the dog. I called to her to stay away, but sure enough she got four or five bees up her skirt in the process. "Oh, they're just rubber bees," she joked for the first couple of minutes in her tough-girl bravado, and then her legs started swelling up and she needed to have some Benadryl too.

The other perpetual risk for runners is dogs, of course. Runners seem an even more attractive target than cats. And it's always the little ones that surprise you. On our loop there are all sorts and sizes, from a black and white Great Dane with floppy ears and one black eye to a pair of hot dog Chihuahuas.

Earlier this summer I felt a charley horse in the back of my thigh as I ran. When I turned around I discovered that a squeamish German shepherd puppy, maybe a year old, had come up behind me and given a halfhearted chomp to the back of my thigh. She was young, but by no means a small dog. I hadn't even seen her coming, and the sneakiness of it pissed me off. I marched right up to the house I thought she came from and told the teenage housewife to train her dog better. The woman apologized and went after the dog with a stick. I could see why the puppy went around biting people, and I regretted squealing on her until a bruise formed on the back of my thigh the next day the size of a small eggplant.

I wrote a poem last year that prophesied that shepherd and the nostalgia I've felt about William all day. I hate having friends like Elizabeth Chu "baby-sit" with William while I pay the bills, answer mail, or try to do some writing. I would love to be cleaning out the garage and arranging his papers, helping him with speech therapy or exercises, or just reading one of the new books publishers are always sending us as review copies. But I have to keep the house running, and I know that I have to take a little time for myself too. The greatest mistake is thinking you can do it all until you wind up worn out or bitter about your fate. But I miss my friend.

When I was looking through the files for that poem I saw again all the hundreds of letters William wrote me in the old days. Exactly fifteen years ago he wrote:

Dear Richard,

It takes an act of will to be happy without you nowadays, but I turn my shoulder blades back (twisting my thumbs outward, is how that's done) and make that act of will. Monday morning is good, after a weekend with you. I love you a lot, brother. You were very dear to me when you patted the nacelle of the airplane and went up the stairs into it yesterday afternoon, you still are and always will be. Never worry about that. It is a source of happiness to me to be able to share you with people, as I did Friday and Saturday and Sunday.

When there are lonely times, call me. Technically is the only way you are ever alone nowadays—I am an annexed part of the Richard syndrome. K went off to town with Mary this morning, and I sleep with the telephone beside my bed whichever house I'm in, so late at night is okay. I think I'll drive to upstate New York Thursday afternoon, to visit my dear old friends the Cases before the Yaddo meeting, but I'll call you off and on. Maybe you'll go to Pennsylvania? When I can't talk to you I write in the blue book. I see you in the news, in the red bomb, having your nose licked by Astra, surrounded by intense young women, liked by a lot of colleagues who would like to have affairs with you, loved by Burt and Dianne and all your inner circle. You're on my retina when my eyes are looking at something or other else.

Have a fine week, William's going to, thanks to you.

yours (am I ever!)
ever,
William

and another thing: while *Chameleon* may need another draft—I think it does, but a fairly mechanical one, to neutralize the sharpness of style—you have, in fact, written a good novel. This has subtly changed your self-assurance. People treat you more seriously and/or lean on you more heavily. It is beautiful to see this. When we have time, let's talk about my reading the book carefully and suggesting the next step. If we could steal a week after New Year's and work here or there in New York. I love you, Richard.

I wish I'd accepted his offer to rewrite the book. I wish I didn't have to find people to entertain him, dream up projects to keep him engaged in life. Here in the country we don't have the resources we have in Washington like the Adult Treatment Center. Before the hospital became sensitive to the issue it used to be called the Adult Day Care Center, and I told him that the minute he didn't find it amusing, the minute he didn't want to be there, we would try something else. But it has proved to be very useful for us both. Three days a week he goes to the hospital and has lunch and various therapies with other stroke victims. Oops, I did it again, "sensationalizing disability," putting the disability before the person. There's a training institute now to help correct outdated and demeaning terms for people who are physically challenged, but the media clichés don't die easily. When you live with someone who has a disability the problem is easier to appreciate. Who wouldn't prefer "uses a wheelchair" to "crippled," or "walks with crutches" instead of "deformed." "Healthy" or "normal" is not the opposite of "disabled," as the institute so rightly points out.

At William's treatment center he's less likely to run into such insensitivity. It's a place where he visits with friends who share his concerns intimately, a place where he can give vent to his generosity by helping those worse off than he is, and mostly it's a place where he doesn't have to work so hard to keep up with the speed of the nondisabled world. But leaving him there isn't any easier than leaving him with Elizabeth Chu.

ADULT TREATMENT CENTER

I

Like a vicious Doberman attacking
out of nowhere as I jog,
the least expected tries again
to spoil the bright morning
I've worked to make our life.

II

The nurse's professional good will
outshines even the sunlight
pouring into the rec hall.
I almost feel like forgetting
the office and sitting down
with you at the art table.

Over Admiral Johnson's shoulder
I inspect today's assignment. He
has chosen a red crayon to fill in
the petals of a single large daisy
xeroxed from a coloring book.
Red wax spills like blood
over the messy page. Any first-
grader would put him to shame.

III

The art therapist hands you
your daisy to color and for
some reason, I see you that
gentle afternoon in Vermont
when you accepted an honorary Ph.D.

Then suddenly there is no stick
to whip him off, no quiet place
by the road to rest. My face
blossoms into a red daisy with
anger. Salt sweat stings my eyes
to tears, when calm and elegant as a
June sky doming the Green Mountains

you turn over the page and begin
to draw from memory a fragile,
but clearly discernible
summer rose of your own.

The remarkable Miss Horn and St. Hubert have saved me, at least for the time being. Yesterday as I let the jets of water wash over my ankle at the college training room my eye caught an article tacked up on the bulletin board comparing various sorts of ankle braces. Later when she was running the ultrasound over my ankle I asked her if she thought a brace might help.

She said the Swede-O Universal was a great brace and asked me if I'd like her to fit me up with it. There are some people who are *born* good. Where did this girl come from?

She laced me into medieval-looking leather braces with plastic stays. There were more eyelets than in a pair of high-top boots your great-grandmother might wear, but by the time they were laced up the white braces blended with my shoes and made me look like I was wearing basketball sneakers. "Wear the braces for four to eight hours to break them in," she said. "The track guys say they don't even know they're wearing them after a while."

In spite of the break-in period, I came back from my run yesterday with blisters on top of the ankle where it bends as you run, exactly like the ones I used to get with my football cleats when I laced them up too tight. But I had managed to run 6.5 miles without having to limp. And this morning I did it again.

Miss Horn has also made me promise to soak the ankles in warm water to warm up the tendons and plantar fascia on the bottom back of the heel where the tendon attaches. After the run I am supposed to ice down the ankle to suppress any bleeding or swelling in the area. For two days this regime has worked, but I don't see how much healing is going to take place. This week I'll go light and then try to come back to where I was in my training when I had to stop.

Karl Ross featured horns in his music program this morning after a full-length mass on "Morning Pro Musica." He played examples of music for the post horn (a Mozart symphony) and the Italian hunting horn (with the unbelievable name of corno da caccia—pronounced "corna gotcha"), and a Kyrie written in honor of St. Hubert, patron saint of the hunt.

The Church is wonderful. Imagine a patron saint for the hunt. I decided that I had to adopt St. Hubert as the patron saint of jogging. Certainly, I'm hunting for victory on November 1. And this morning I was chased twice by dogs as I ran, once by the aforementioned shepherd puppy, then by a new dog, a dalmation of some age, visiting down at one of the new modular "Contempri-Homes" that are springing up like mushrooms after a rain on the lower marina road. The shepherd turned around fast this time when she saw who I was, and the dalmation I was able to stop cold with my standard technique: plant yourself, make a fast, sharp pointing motion to his head, and scream with as much authority as you can muster, "You go home!" If the owner is around, you can also scream, "Leash law, leash law!" The dog won't know the difference, but the owner might get the point. St. Hubert won't hold it against you.

"Maybe I ought to be praying to St. Jude," I said to Martha when she finished her lesson with William and agreed to stay for lunch.

"Now which one is he? I'm not very up on the saints," she said with a certain amount of pride in that fact.

"He's the patron saint of hopeless causes," I explained.

"Mercy," she said. "Why doesn't everybody go to *him* right away?"

Martha had a good appetite at lunch, loved the final course of honeydew melon with honey vanilla Häagen Daz. *"No one* appreciates ice cream the way they should," she said in the wonderful way she has of proclaiming things.

"Except the wise children," I reminded her.

"Into the mouths of babes. Quite right."

She did us a final service before leaving. William, always the cat lover, has taken to one of the kittens here, and we've decided to take it back to D.C. when we leave. It is a bold thing, exactly the blond yellow color Mikey sports. It doesn't hesitate a minute to eat out of the dog's dish or jump up on the stove if it smells something good. There is trouble in store, but we've decided to take him. We'd been calling him Toscanini, Tosca for short, and today Martha brought him some catnip to get him started. She thinks he should be called Kitemaug, the Indian name of one of the streets in her village. The street is pronounced "Kitty maug," however, and so it shall be. After the marathon me, Mikey, William, and Kittymaug will load up the Volvo and head south with the geese.

On the train again, headed to New York for a plane to Phoenix and San Diego, William asleep at my side. The foliage is spectacular as we head south, some of the trees a day-glow pink. I'll miss running my familiar loop, and Ann won't be around to help with William in the morning. But the whole point of this trip is to have a change of pace after a long summer of routine. And dear baby sister Jude and the nephews. It will be good to visit them again. Poor Mikey, so forlorn as we packed our bags. I gave him a private lecture and told him to be good till we get home.

The weather is clearing after yesterday's downpour. My ankle is very sore after my run, but so far my plan of training through the injury till race day is working. I set out three mugs of water in the mailbox Sunday morning, but couldn't promise myself that I would make it four times around the loop. Saturday was a very odd day, with too much drinking. A friend's granddaughter got married, and the whole family was split over the marriage. The bride told her father he couldn't come to the wedding, and half the family wouldn't go until she changed her mind and apologized. Very sticky to walk the line between two camps. The only nice touch of the day was watching the girl's godmother speak to her as we left the reception. She looked into the eyes of her goddaughter, both of them crying, the bride in a peasant bridal gown, pearls sprayed about her veil and face, the godmother like a portly Melina Mercouri in leopard dress and turban. "Make your husband be good to your children," she said to the beautiful girl in an effort to draw a lesson from the unfortunate controversy.

Sunday morning, hungover spiritually and physically, the rain stripping the trees of their leaves, it did not seem possible to try my first big run in several weeks. But I put out three cups of water anyway, and like an Alcoholics Anonymous member who mustn't think about "the rest of his life," I started off the morning one loop at a time.

I am in the first loop, I chant as I go, later I will be in the third loop, later I will be icing the ankle down and then I will take a hot shower. Time will pass and all this will happen. Just now, though, I am in the first loop. I am warm and content inside my red L.L. Bean slicker. My legs are naked trunks hanging from the red slicker, they are muscular, brown, as well shaped as a professional soccer player's. I can't believe they are mine. I take the most comfortable chair in the room under the hood of my red slicker where Susan Stamberg begins interviewing various guests on her "Weekend Edition" radio program. Mary McCarthy talks about her recent book and quotes George Orwell. If an autobiography doesn't include something an author is ashamed of, it isn't much of a book. What will my admission be? Perhaps my habit of ruminating on some real or imagined offense, reviewing it in the context of the three conditions of mortal sin, going through weeks of obsessive introspection. Betty sent me a Garfield cartoon once where he is pushing a stupid rabbit off a cliff. "The only way to deal with a free-floating guilt complex," Garfield says, "is to do something that deserves it."

Last week I had pretty much decided to fly up to Montreal for a few days and shop for fur coats for me and William. We'd been there once with Mom and Dad, and it seemed to be the fur capital of the world. Sometimes cabin fever and self-pity and boredom build up and I have to have a little treat, do something a little crazy to prove to myself that I'm free, or that life isn't passing me by.

Langston Hughes once complimented William when he wore his best studs at a formal occasion. "I like to see a poet wearing *diamonds,*" Hughes told William. This winter I'd like to turn up wearing fur coats. I want us to keep warm, I want people to say, "Get a load of these guys." This week Alice and Dave sent us plush wool tams from their summer trip to Scotland, red plaid for me, blue-green for William. Soft, thick, lush. They *require* fur coats. I've been cutting advertisements all week from the *New York Times.* I figure I'll save at least a thousand dollars by skipping Montreal.

This morning as I ran through Central Park I couldn't help thinking about the furs. The weather was bright but blustery cold, really a winter day. The coats made me warm just day-dreaming about them. I wish we had had them when we went to Bulgaria two years ago, during the month of April. When we got off the little jet bringing us from Paris to Sophia old-fashioned camera bulbs popped and children approached, shyly, burdened with bouquets of roses. The American Vaptsarov winner was returning to Bulgaria, where poetry is a popular art form and football stadiums overflow with poetry lovers if one of the arch-angels comes to town. Here the head of the Writer's Union holds the rank of cabinet member, and the vice-president is a poet. William's return was a media event, especially since his illness had made the trip even more of a special effort for him. All the dignitaries were lined up, the black limousines waiting. There was no effort to disguise special treatment. Even the lug-gage came through with big red and white VIP tags that I've only seen on Balkan Air Lines. We poked our head out of the plane and then gingerly made our way down the red carpet. A number of poets, burly as black bears, were crying openly to see their old friend again. Only problem was that spring comes two months later in this part of the world, and we would up freezing our butts off from the Pirin Mountains to the Black Sea.

Once at the Academy Institute when Erskine Caldwell was being inducted, I was describing what fantastic lithography was being done by the young artists at Varna to a luncheon guest. A woman walked by and proclaimed with the conviction of an Old Testament prophet, "You're all being used. Cheever, Meredith. You're all being used."

We had just come back from the Fifth International Meeting of Writers in Bulgaria, where Mr. Caldwell was the honorary chairman of the meeting, so her comment I found a little abra-sive. But the response was not unique. She isn't the first to raise an eyebrow about our travels behind the "iron curtain."

This past March when I finally got William home from all his operations in Florida, I received a call from an FBI agent who wanted to talk with me. He wouldn't discuss what he wanted, but when I pressed him he said it concerned where I had parked my car. I did a wild and rapid review of my life the past six weeks in Miami. Mostly I'd been at the hospital, but a couple of nights I went to a gay bar and met some people. God knows where I'd parked my car in the drug capital of the world.

Two beefy agents, mid-forties, well dressed, all-American, sat down in the living room and explained that William and I had been photographed going into the Bulgarian embassy last September carrying some packages. Could I please explain what our business there was? I believe I asked them if I *had* to explain my business, and when they said no I was far more inclined to speak with them.

On occasion William sends signed copies of books by American masters to the Writer's Union, I said. They are classic books in contemporary literature that the Bulgarian people might never see or have access to. The Bulgarians are so grateful they have set up a special room in the National Library to house the collection. All simple cultural exchange, all very innocent, I explained.

A few more questions and they made a polite farewell. One can understand the need for such sleuthing in the abstract, but it's a little unsettling to think you have a file somewhere in the FBI records. What *else* might be in there?

As a health officer for Westinghouse in the old days, I traveled from Morocco to the Philippines, Bamako to Pusan, with projects such as nuclear power plants and air force radar systems. I learned to keep my nose clean and assume the walls had ears. A company executive I was traveling with in west Africa explained to me once that my chauffeur might indeed be the tribal prince still hiding from Western ways, and that the man on the throne might be some flunky installed by the real chief. You assumed your conversation was being monitored in ministerial waiting rooms. But even in the good old USA you had to wonder if you could always assume fair play from the CIA or FBI after Watergate and Iran-gate.

William's feeling about traveling to the Eastern Bloc has always been that if poets and writers can't speak to one another across political and cultural barriers, there isn't much hope for politicians or anyone else. Clearly the Russians must foot the bill for such international writers' conferences as a way of lobbying against cruise missile deployment in Europe, or whatever particular goal they have at the time. But American artists are not naive about such matters. And William has given the most beautiful defense of our system, our way of life, to the Eastern Block artists, one that even the Great Communicator Ronald Reagan couldn't begin to match.

As long as the Bulgarians support the positions the Russians espouse on a global scale, they are given extraordinary freedom to live their everyday lives pretty much as they wish, it seems. It is a productive country, the breadbasket for Russia, a kind of little Switzerland with mountains, vineyards, European architecture. Their writers drink, make love, and engage in artistic politics just like American writers. They tend to spoil their children and hope, the same way we do, that our leaders don't blow up the planet.

There are differences, of course. Once, in Varna, our host told the story of a little boy who found a golden ring among the ruins of the Roman baths there. The little boy promptly took the ring to the museum as any socially conscious citizen would. His parents and the community didn't even think twice about the normalcy of his act.

I had to say I found this a little hard to believe—that maybe a boy's *parents* might march him in to do the right thing, but that any boy I knew would consider it lost booty and stick it on his finger. Their notion of social responsibility to the state was a cultural ideal that I simply couldn't believe was real, and finally I had to stop discussing it or risk ruining the trip. I still thought America the best country in the world. Dog eat dog, yes, violent and often cruel, but relatively free.

This morning's run in Central Park was my first since the Tune-Up, and it felt good to be "home." Nothing like a crisp day in Manhattan to get your adrenalin going. Already the sides of buses were plastered with welcoming messages for the New

York City Marathon from insurance and liquor companies, and blue and white banners were flying over the lanes in the park to mark the course.

The women walking the streets wore silk blouses and miniskirts, which had come into fashion again this year, shorter than ever. The young hunks heading to Wall Street gave me casual glances, wondering how I managed to be running at the start of business hours, envying that luxury a little maybe. So far my strategy was holding. I had run through the pain without limping, and already it was time to go back to the apartment. *Running* the marathon and not just doing the marathon seemed possible for the first time in days.

A generation ago orchards used to separate the little towns that dotted the valley, and when you went from one to the other you had the sense of leaving and returning home. Now a megalopolis spreads nonstop like Los Angeles under the purple dome of Arizona sky, with grids of streets and freeways, perpetual construction, and air that has the newly won distinction of being some of the dirtiest in the country. Except for the occasional concession to a Spanish heritage, mostly glass towers rise up on the boulevards, with chain stores and fast food franchises mushrooming below. You could be *anywhere* in America, except perhaps for the palm trees. Even the radio stations play the same hard rock or easy listening music that is piped into elevators and shopping malls. When the snowbirds come the population swells by the thousands, and it may take an hour to cross town. For half of the year the temperature is oppressive, and people move from air-conditioned house to car to office. There are two million people in the valley now, and the town has swollen into the ninth largest city in America.

You might not think Phoenix the ideal city to live in, but it has become a mecca for the upwardly mobile and retirees alike. There seems to be something of a real estate gold rush going on, and the unemployment rate is below the national average. Neither of these facts will keep our hosts here anymore, though. In August the house they have lived in for ten years was broken into for the fourth time. Lee says this has nothing to do with their decision, but by the time this book is out they will have moved to Santa Fe. Stewart says he doesn't like his air conditioned, and despite the fact that the Udall family has been here for generations, they have had enough "progress."

These old friends of William's go back to the time William and Robert Frost were traveling cross-country and stopped in Tucson. Stewart asked William if Frost would go for the idea of reading at Kennedy's inauguration, and William thought it a great idea. They've been fast friends ever since. Stewart feels that only he and William and Theodore Morrison can talk of the rift between Kennedy and Frost at the end of their lives, and he means some day to correct the record. Who, he ponders, would have thought at the outset that the old poet and young president would die in the same year? Udall is a lover of poetry and one of the few public men who, in recent memory, have even appreciated the possible use of this art form in public life. When he was secretary of the interior he suggested to President Johnson that William's poem commemorating the wreck of the submarine *Thresher* be sent to the surviving family members on the first anniversary of the tragedy, but Johnson, it seems, was disinclined to imitate Kennedy in anything, and the idea was rejected.

Stewart and William both have a well-developed sense of their public identity. Both can be stuffy, especially at a formal dinner party or on ceremonial occasions, but William's poem, I think, is one of the few fine *public* poems in contemporary poetry.

THE WRECK OF THE THRESHER
(lost at sea, April 10, 1963)

I stand on the ledge where rock runs into the river
As the night turns brackish with morning, and mourn the drowned.
Here the sea is diluted with river; I watch it slaver
Like a dog curing of rabies. Its ravening over,
Lickspittle ocean nuzzles the dry ground.
(But the dream that woke me was worse than the sea's grey
Slip-slap; there are no such sounds by day.)

This crushing of people is something we live with.
Daily, by unaccountable whim
Or caught up in some harebrained scheme of death,
Tangled in cars, dropped from the sky, in flame,
Men and women break the pledge of breath:
And now under water, gone all jetsam and small
In the pressure of oceans collected, a squad of brave men in a hull.

(Why can't our dreams be content with the terrible facts?
The only animal cursed with responsible sleep,
We trace disaster always to our own acts.
I met a monstrous self trapped in the black deep:
All these years, he smiled, *I've drilled at sea*
For this crush of water. Then he saved only me.)

We invest ships with life. Look at a harbor
At first light: with better grace than men
In their movements the vessels run to their labors
Working the fields that the tide has made green again;
Their beauty is womanly, they are named for ladies and queens,
Although by a wise superstition these are called
After fish, the finned boats, silent and submarine.
The crushing of any ship has always been held
In dread, like a house burned or a great tree felled.

I think of how sailors laugh, as if cold and wet
And dark and lost were their private, funny derision
And I can judge then what dark compression
Astonishes them now, their sunken faces set
Unsmiling, where the currents sluice to and fro
And without humor, somewhere northeast of here and below.

(Sea-brothers, I lower to you the ingenuity of dreams,
Strange lungs and bells to escape in; let me stay aboard last—
We amend our dreams in half-sleep. Then it seems
Easy to talk to the severe dead and explain the past.
Now they are saying, *Do not be ashamed to stay alive,*
You have dreamt nothing that we do not forgive.
And gentlier, *Study something deeper than yourselves,*
As, how the heart, when it turns diver, delves and saves.)

Whether we give assent to this or rage
Is a question of temperament and does not matter.
Some will has been done past our understanding,
Past our guilt surely, equal to our fears.
Dullards, we are set again to the cryptic blank page
Where the sea schools us with terrible water.
The noise of a boat breaking up and its men is in our ears.
The bottom here is too far down for our sounding;
The ocean was salt before we crawled to tears.

Stewart maneuvered the Chevy Blazer through heavy traffic and grumbled that Phoenix was one of the few cities in America that still had its airport in the very center of town. Santa Fe, on the other hand, was unspoiled.

Years ago they had bought land in the New Mexico foothills for retirement, and now they would give up their little hacienda in the old section of downtown Phoenix and rebuild. Cultural life was rich in Santa Fe, social life more intimate. You found fewer new rich folk throwing their money around. And it was much cooler there.

I told him of my time at Camp Philmont in New Mexico, the 380,000-acre ranch that the Phillips family had donated to the Boy Scouts of America outside of Cimarron City. At age fourteen I had won an essay contest on "Why I want to go to Camp Philmont," and traveled across the country for the first time all by myself.

"What did you write?" Stewart asked.

"I told them that I wanted to go to get skills that I could share with my brother scouts. Sheer self-sacrifice, mind you. But you know, the funny thing is that I did become an Explorer scout and took younger scouts on canoe trips to Canada for a number of years after that. Philmont was terrific."

"Beautiful country."

"But hot. It was so hot I was practically in a coma. For days I just bobbed around on my burro, offering up the heat for the souls in purgatory. I was reading Thomas Merton's book about becoming a Cistercian monk. Do you know the *Seven Storey Mountain?*"

"Uh-huh."

"Well, I could feel God's *presence* in those desert mountains. We were doing archeology as one of our merit badges, and I wound up on a dig that was investigating this Spanish sect that crucified some member of the community each holy season. I mean they literally nailed them to a cross until death."

"The Penitentes."

"That's right. We actually dug up the crucifixes they used. I was about as clearheaded as Joan of Arc and thought it was wonderful. I even had something of a mystical experience of my own."

Stewart was interested in anything that had to do with the out-of-doors. He drove with his head tilted like RCA Victor's dog. I knew he was listening intensely. As a boy Stewart had completed two years of the mandatory missionary work required of Mormons, but it was only after he defied the elders and refused to give up his belief in racial equality that he came to terms with the excesses of his religion.

"We'd been on a long night hike," I said, "and I forgot and left my tent at a rest stop about a mile before we made camp. The scoutmaster said I would have to go back by myself and get it. Well, throughout the trip we had seen rattlesnakes and even a bear, and I was scared. In ten minutes I had wandered off the trail and was totally frantic. I heard all sorts of noises and was sure I'd get eaten up or never find my way back. I sat under a thorn bush and cried for a while, then I prayed to the Virgin and made some promises, if she would only let me find my way home. The sky was brilliant with stars, and when my eyes had gotten a little more used to the dark, and the prayer calmed me down some, I got up and like a sleepwalker went directly to my tent and back up the mountain. I pitched my tent and had a deep, dreamless sleep. I mean, I know this can all be explained in terms of simple psychology. All I had to do was collect my thoughts and slow down the adrenalin a bit. But at the time I was sure a miracle had occurred."

"You had a very dumb scoutmaster," was all Stewart said. But he was no stranger to the desert and wouldn't scoff at the idea of a desert miracle.

Some years ago the Heard Museum took him up on the idea of retracing the route Coronado had followed in search of the seven cities of gold and invited him to lead a bus trip to retrace the old trail. Why, he felt, should East Coast bluebloods emote so over their colonial forefathers when Spanish conquistadores were exploring the West and setting up missions hundreds of years before the Bradfords and Smiths got to New England? In one generation the Spanish had annexed more land than the entire Roman Empire. There had never been a period like it before in history, yet for some reason America chooses to ignore its Hispanic heritage.

Stewart thought of a book that would follow one such explorer and even examine Spain's incredible age of discovery. He wrote a note to Jackie Onassis at Doubleday, and she came west to see the land and discuss the idea. Three years later he had produced a killer coffee table book, *To the Inland Empire,* and William and I had had the luck now to turn up the very week of its publication. It was like visiting a household under the golden spell of a new baby.

After dinner we sat under the stars in the backyard catching up on our lives. Stewart's pipe illuminated his face as he smoked. His black eyes were bright as an animal's shining in the night. The talk was serious. Frost in the old days, his brother's Parkinson's disease, his hopes for William's progress. Stewart would have to leave in the morning for a conference on energy in Boulder, and he saw William too infrequently to waste words.

Before we all went to bed they inscribed the book for us, Stewart pressing his wife to sign his work with him. It was more than just a courtly bow to his helpmate, though, since she works closely as his editor. Lee is not the usual political wife standing like an acolyte at the altar of her husband's career. She's wonderfully sassy and smiles right through any attempt to bulldoze her. But clearly she is as proud to have the new book out after all these years as Stewart is.

One of the nice things about jogging is that you can take the sport with you easily wherever you go. No need for fancy equipment, teammates, or a special playing field. You just put on your shoes and start running. It is a wonderful way to discover a new town. No one pays any attention to you, not even muggers usually, and in the most secretive cities in the world you can often jog right into places that normally would be forbidden or at least require a guide. The natives might think you're crazy, but they are rarely hostile. And you can get into parts of the town where a tour bus can't go.

I loved running in Phoenix. The air didn't seem any worse to me than New York's. And everywhere you looked red mountains lined the valley and called you into the desert. On foot I was able to see the cactus gardens surrounding the office buildings, sneak up on high school students smoking marijuana before classes, and window shop for everything from Western ties to custom bikinis.

When I had run for half an hour down Third Street, I came to the canals of the Salt River, clear, sky-blue water running smack into town from the mountains with bike paths on either side of the clay embankments. The little river ran through a poor section of town where people raised a few cattle or kept chickens. Dogs skulked around trying to avoid the rabies patrol trucks that prowled the neighborhood. There were no manicured lawns here, only dusty fields under the oleander bushes. A lot of friends from the old days did their graduate work in Tucson, and I imagined them living in this sort of student housing, smoking dope, drinking tequila sunrises, blown away on the Eagles or Bob Dylan.

Lee and William would just be finishing their breakfast when I got back, deep into some reminiscence of their old days. Lee is one of the friends who is particularly patient and has an easy time with William's disability. She is able to fill in the awkward pauses with questions and wait till the thread of his thought becomes evident so that he never feels pressed to come up with a name or some word that is blocking the conversation. He enjoyed their conversation so much he would stay in his bathrobe till lunch.

Once when he had gone up for his shower and I was finishing the third orange juice freshly squeezed from oranges in their garden, Lee talked to me about William's illness in an oblique way. She spoke of a married couple that was having a hard time because of the invalid wife's attitude. At age seventy she still insisted that only her husband could care for her, and so he spent the last years of his life exhausted with such care. They could afford outside help, but she insisted that he do the work.

Lee explained that she and Stewart had a pact that "whoever fell over first" would not be a burden to the other if the healthy partner still had a productive life remaining. They had worked it out ahead of time so that they wouldn't be consumed by guilt if nurses were required for care. It might even result in a better life for both of them, she reasoned.

I'm sure this was her diplomatic way of suggesting that I not feel obliged to do it all for William, and I was grateful for that concern for *me* in all this as well. Sometimes friends who have known William for a lifetime and me for only a while take umbrage that we have a housekeeper who does the laundry and will even cook our lunches for us, as though that should be my duty for the rest of my adult life. It is only their love for William, of course, that accounts for their blinders in this regard, but it is wonderful to have friends who are able to see what life is like for both of us. It had only been a couple of days, we'd only visited a museum and the botanical gardens, but when Lee dropped us at the airport and made us promise to come back in the spring, I felt happier than I had in a long time and realized how important the past few days had been.

My friend Betty sometimes annoys me when I can't coax her into some project that involves a number of people she knows only slightly. There are so many folks she loves dearly and it is so difficult to see them all, she doesn't like to waste time. You run the risk of getting a little too insular with this sort of attitude, but our visit to Phoenix was so rich I began to see her point. If life gets lonely out on the river, jump on a plane or into your car and follow your heart.

For three days we have been luxuriating at the Princess Resort, forty-three acres of rather silly Polynesian bungalows, restaurants, and swimming pools stuck right in the middle of the bay here in San Diego. Like anyone else who has to keep up his professional certification, I try to schedule educational conferences in cities where I can visit with friends or vacation in a town I've never been to before. This time I've brought William along with me to "Office Orthopedics for the Primary Care Physician," and the extracurricular pleasure I've worked into the trip is a chance to visit with baby sister Jude and her family, who have expatriated out here. William's niece has also settled on the West Coast, and we've been able to visit with her too.

I wish I felt better about this "paradise" they now call home. Everything is so clean and sunny and laid back. Everybody so tan. It's unnatural. I feel like a Neil Simon character who has just stepped off the plane bundled up in his winter overcoat, gray, pasty, eyes adjusting to the bright light with great difficulty.

The clichés about the East Coast versus the West are about as old as our country's history, I suppose, the debate going back as far as Tocqueville. And if you looked deep enough, the differences would no doubt turn out to be only superficial, but on the surface, at least, they seem to hold.

Go west, young man, push on to new lands and golden opportunity. Escape the stultifying East, with its uptight, class-conscious, puritan-ridden social structure. Take off your tie and put on a bathing suit. Surf's up. This is the cutting edge of American culture, what we are about to become. No one's going to judge you for trying something new. No one's going to tell you what to do anymore, not your parents, not the Church, not the Joneses next door. Just do your thing, and, hey, enjoy.

The visitor from Manhattan looks around at all the wide open spaces and the mellow natives zooming along eight-lane freeways like a particularly bright rat who has been let into a clean, well-lighted storehouse for the American Cheese Company.

He's suspicious of the democratic easiness, the obsession with health and fitness, the egalitarian rootlessness of it all. Like, who *are* these valley girls? Does Bar-Bar-Bar-Bar-Bar Barbara Ann really have *anything* on her mind? William's niece was clear about it. Like, L.A. was her town, and her mother could keep New York with all its pushing and shoving. All she wanted was a hot car and an open road.

And my own sister too was happy to be out from under all the deadwood that had weighed her down. She had tried to make the East work. For two years when she and her husband were stationed in San Diego we heard nothing but how wonderful it would be to return to Pennsylvania, buy a house, and settle down to real life. And when John got out of the navy everyone in the family pitched in and made their dream house become a reality like neighbors come to help raise a barn.

A year after they moved in, of course, they longed to return to California. People didn't *do* anything in York, Pennsylvania, except maybe go to Ocean City two weeks out of the year in the summer, and sit at home gossiping about their neighbors for the other fifty. Raising her babies under the watchful eye of mother and sisters put her constantly at odds with the family, when *she* was the one who had earned a degree in early childhood development from Connecticut College's distinguished program. She and John longed for the immediate social acceptance that is a kind of self-defense mechanism that goes along with military life. The kids had grown accustomed to going barefoot most of the year, they missed their friends at the zoo. There were no more spring camping trips into the desert. The way sassafras only grows east of the Rockies, they seemed to need another climate in which to bloom.

Returning to California was probably the hardest thing she ever did in her life, because everyone saw her leaving as a kind of betrayal. She would be "out there" for good now, would have to sleep in the bed she had made. When the holidays rolled around she would just have to invite her new friends and neighbors in for Thanksgiving or Christmas turkey. Grandma would make an effort to visit when she could, but wouldn't be able to watch the grandchildren grow and spoil them when they lived thousands of miles away. They would turn into little "beach boys," blond and beautiful and of a certain brainlessness. They might not go to Harvard, but they would be visually literate, vaguely apolitical, perfect physical specimens and a lot less hung up on "self," New Age prototypes for the evolutionary leap Teilhard de Chardin says we are on the verge of making. And they would rarely think of uncles and aunts from the past "back East."

Of course, what she was doing was no different from what our mother had done when she eloped with our father and moved away from the coal fields of western Pennsylvania. The Bible spells it out: "A man will leave his family and cling to his wife. . . ." She was simply a different generation, setting up her little brood with the man she loved, inventing her own family traditions. It was all very understandable. But her decision to move back to San Diego saddened everyone deeply in spite of how logical it might be. It seemed as though her family were going into self-imposed exile.

Judy and I had been so close all the years our family moved around from one little town in Pennsylvania to the next, my only best friend as we went from one school system to the next. Her leaving us was something like the death of the family unit for me, the official end of my youth. It might be inexorable, but it wasn't any more acceptable than any other sort of goodbye one had to make in life.

Last Easter Judy sent us a videotape of her appearance on a TV show called "Baby Talk." There she was, tan and ten pounds trimmer, speaking to a group of mothers spread out on on the floor playing with their babies in front of the camera. She used all the scientific jargon that describes when a baby develops control of its head and stops bobbing around like a sunflower, what the newborn baby is and isn't seeing in the early weeks of life, which neurological reflexes will develop next. But she also talked about what to do when baby won't take a pacifier, how to handle jealousy from the firstborn, kibitzing with humor and authority and compassion with these teenage mothers who were living lonely military lives in San Diego and didn't have their own mothers around to give them tips about raising children.

The whole family sat without saying anything after the video-tape was over, musing on the fact that good old Jude had sort of made it, had probably been right in doing what she had to do all along. Mother has since made copies of the tape for all her friends in the neighborhood. Recipes are now flowing from coast to coast again.

It's Judy's theory that San Diego is the gateway to the Pacific Basin, and that in no time at all flying to see her will be as commonplace as driving to Ocean City in the summer. The world is going to get smaller and smaller as technology develops—very California, this—and if the older generations in the family remain reluctant, at least nieces and nephews will begin to turn up from time to time to participate in her life. Here I was, after all, just come out for a medical conference, easy as you please.

Still, it will be very hard to leave her at the airport for all her bravado. And hard too to say goodbye to John and the nephews. Ian and Liam—Irish for William, his namesake—were such cute little bugs these past few days, swimming under the water-falls, exploring the island on a four-wheel bicycle buggy with a fringe on top, lecturing me on dinosaurs. When I see them next, they'll likely have moved on to other games.

The conference has been pretty interesting, though, with catchy topical lectures such as "Whiplash, and Other Pains in the Neck" (knew a lawyer once who had a yacht called *Whip-lash*), "A Medical Approach to the Hot Joint," and "Hand Problems: Don't Lose Your Grip." The only "pearl" I got out of "Ankle Injuries—Ace, Brace, Tape, Cast, or Cut?" was the mild encouragement to "run through" an injury within reason by using a nonsteroidal anti-inflammatory medication, Advil, say, or some other over-the-counter equivalent before beginning the run. By cutting down the inflammation I'd decrease the swelling and pain and continue to use the joint during training. I might train and still not risk the healing process too much, with luck.

Sunday morning I thought I'd give it a try, since my schedule called for one of the longer runs in the training—the last long run, in fact, before the marathon—and my ankle was still an iffy proposition. In spite of the aches and pains, however, I had to admit to myself that regardless of what happened I had come a long way. I asked the guy at the front desk what might be a good course to run a long training run, and when he told me it was seventeen miles around the bay I didn't give it a second thought. Weeks ago I couldn't have managed seven miles, and now I was going to try seventeen.

It was misty and still cool yesterday morning at ten when I ran out of the gate of Princess Village. William promised he would go back to bed after I gave him his medications and that he would hang around the bungalow watching the morning news shows until I got back. I had the early part of the day to myself, and the bay lay sweet and shimmering, waiting for me.

Sunday mornings in San Diego the natives take their rest as they do everywhere else in the country. I suppose. Several party animals lay scattered around the bonfire ashes in the park, sleeping off last night's revelry, as I crossed the bridge connecting our island to the mainland. A couple of fishermen lounged along the rail, and a single water-skier made his slow way past the lighthouse in the distance. Far across the bay I could just make out the tiny peninsula that would be the midpoint in the run. I realized that I probably should have checked out the course with the car before trying this run, but sometimes as you ran you had to go places a car simply couldn't go. Once I hit the coast all I had to do was follow the shoreline and keep certain landmarks in view. The course looked roughly like the head of a cockroach when I tried to imagine where my run would take me.

It was already warming up as I reached the shore, and I regretted wearing my jacket. Two guys came up the street running bareback, and both said Hi as they passed. In San Diego, at least, runners greeted one another. In Central Park you'd think all the joggers were deaf-mutes. Every day this week I had run across another jogger who just accepted it as natural that we would run together a while and chat. Yesterday a nice old guy used the pretext that he was wearing the same Saucony shoes as I to strike up a conversation. He liked them because they controlled his

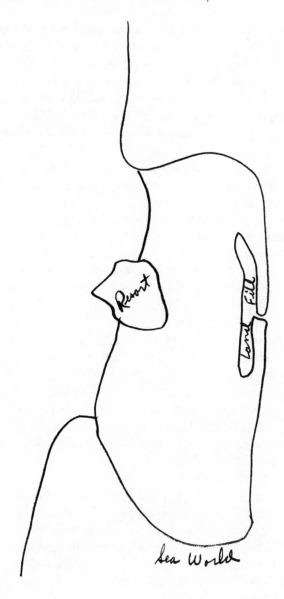

pronating as he ran. I recounted all the tips I got at the conference, told him my plans to run a final big run tomorrow in my marathon training. He congratulated me with the kind of reverence that I had felt for long-distance runners only a few months ago. Now I was the one giving assurances that he could try a marathon, that it wasn't as difficult as one might think. Noblesse oblige. Nice, the easy self-confidence this sort of training was building in me.

Yesterday the Associated Writing Programs tracked us down at the hotel to invite us to their spring convention in San Francisco where a tribute is to be given by a number of poets in William's honor. I had to put my foot down in a way that was a little pushy, even for me, to get the program right. I've always hated a certain self-importance in some writers my age, but at some point you have to begin to take yourself and your work seriously or nobody else does. Instead of opening doors, living close to a famous writer often makes you go out of your way to avoid any *hint* of nepotism, and many opportunities are left to die on the vine. I care a lot less about how things look to the world the older I get. Running has helped me here, I think, for better or worse.

As I ran past the houses and apartment buildings overlooking the bay with their fountains and swimming pools and walls of glass, I had to admit that this was very beautiful country, though I wouldn't want to own a house on these cliffs when "the big one" came. The natives, of course, discounted summer earthquakes as episodes of "shake and bake."

"You gotta go sometime," William's niece, Susie, said, lighting a cigarette at the end of dinner when we all went out last night, "whether it's an airplane, an earthquake, or lung cancer." Maybe the fatalism of living on a fault line accounts for Californians' proverbial nonchalance, like well-adjusted lemmings drinking wine coolers at the cliff's edge overlooking the Pacific.

"Do you work here?" I had asked the young woman who seemed to be a waitress after we had waited fifteen minutes for someone to show us a menu.

"Yeah, sometimes. Ha, ha, ha," she said. She looked as though she might sit down and join us for a drink.

Susie thought me pretty stuffy, of course, when I complained about the woman's approach to customers—I was a good example of the kind of snobbery she had left behind her in the East, no doubt. I thought of Frost's notion that free verse was like playing tennis without a net. In California they had taken down all the nets.

"I've done all kinds of work in my life, Susie," I said. "I've carried my share of bed pans and I even hauled garbage one summer. But when I eat out in a restaurant I want a waitress to treat me like the public, not like family. Just a little polite distance."

"Crab, crab, crab, Richard," Susie laughed. She patted my cheek. And, of course, after the first martini, the waitress turned out to be more charming than Audrey Hepburn and wound up with a fat, guilty tip by the time we finished our Irish coffee.

One sure way of finding a good course to run in a strange city is to follow a local jogger, and for a while I trailed behind the trim little guy who came prancing out of Campland on the Bay. He was blond-haired, nut brown, and weighed about 160 pounds, just about what I ought to weigh ideally. It was as though the mythical thin man who is supposed to exist inside every fat man had jumped out and was pacing me around the bay.

We ran by what must surely have been a gay apartment building. Ten guys hung out on the steps showing off their tan torsos, listening to music, drinking beer. They scrutinized a young Adonis in cutoffs who worked bent over the hood of his old Corvette across the street, oblivious of his admirers.

I began to feel a little homesick as we jogged on the other side of a fence running along the local golf course. Retired couples teed up for their Sunday morning game the way Mom and Dad had undoubtedly done on the East Coast a few hours earlier. The golfers chatted quietly, pleasantly, with one another and took warm-up swings. The men razzed each other about their

shots, the women sat in the carts gossiping about this and that
while waiting their turns. How many Sunday mornings had I
started off the day just this way with Mom and Dad? Soon they
would be heading to Florida for the winter. Judy hadn't con-
vinced them to try California this year even though she billed
San Diego as the golf capital of the West. They had their own
friends at Daytona who would be waiting for them. We
wouldn't see the snowbirds until next spring.

The seaside park extending along much of the bay was now
coming alive with bike riders, wind surfers, and families out for a
Sunday picnic. Children played on charming toys fashioned to
look like seals, turtles, and baby whales, teaching them to love
the sea. Mile markers were painted on the sidewalk for joggers.
One family, including three generations, came riding by with
babies wearing miniature crash helmets strapped into the rear
seats attached to the bikes. Hundreds of strange little birds
pecked at the ground like domesticated chickens. They had gray
bodies, black heads, and white beaks, something like designer
pigeons. I'd never seen such creatures and made a mental note to
look them up in Audubon when I got home. They flew away in
unison when a bicycle raced by but settled again just a few feet
away. The biker was a pretty strange bird himself, actually: gray-
haired, wearing a woman's low-cut, single-piece, electric-blue
body stocking with red and gold stripes running down the leg.
Wonderful. Only in California.

An hour and a half into the run the beautiful park petered out
and the runner I'd been following turned off into the parking lot
of the Hilton Hotel. A huge Mississippi-style paddleboat waited
in the bay to take on guests for Sunday brunch. Shortly, the
landscape got a lot less fancy and the shoreline resembled the
terrain of a construction site. It was difficult to run without
stumbling on ruts and uneven sidewalks. When I came to the
paved road that turned off onto the peninsula I stopped for a
moment and asked a man walking his dog how far it was around
the stretch of land and back to the entrance. He looked at me as
though I were a little crazy but said he supposed it was three or
four miles.

The "island" was deserted and completely naked of any vege-
tation. Occasionally I would come across a beat-up old Cadillac
or van parked off to the side, the owners out of sight. Once I did
see a long-haired character who looked like a movie extra for
Woodstock or the *Texas Chainsaw Massacre.* I imagined the
dark cars full of addicts shooting heroin and began looking over
my shoulder every now and then as the landscape became more
barren, more remote. When I had run about a mile and a half it
became clear why the guy with the dog had looked at me funny
when I asked for directions. The foul stench I noticed when I
first came on the peninsula had become so strong it was now
almost visible as I ran. Apparently, I was running on a huge
garbage dump that would someday stop stinking and become an
expensive "landfill" reclamation project. Houses costing God
knows how much would be built on top of twenty years' worth of
poison and filth. I'd gone more than halfway, so it made no sense
to turn back at this point. Ahead, a man stood beside the road in
the deserted terrain shouting at his wife and dog. He used the
same tone of voice for both. He wasn't hitting her, but she stood
there dumb like the animal, as though he might. When I passed
by I said Hi, and the man bared his teeth and actually snarled at
me. A drizzle of rain began that made the thinly covered garbage
smell ten times worse. The rancid mist soaked my skin and permeated my clothes. When I finally came to the entrance again
and headed toward the fine needlepoint tower of Sea World at
the far end of the bay, I felt like Dorothy coming to the end of
the yellow brick road into Oz.

My course turned into a four-lane highway now, and since
there was no sidewalk through the high weeds growing in ruts
alongside the road, I was forced to run on the berm. Cars and
tractor trailers came zooming by, laying on the horn. They came
close enough to blow me off the road once or twice. My ankle
hurt too much now to try sprinting, but I managed to get across
the congested entrances to Sea World, where parents were
speeding the little darlings to spend an afternoon with Shamu
the killer whale. All that mellow California tolerance you hear
about evaporates when the natives get into their cars. On free-

ways it's every man for himself, and lately some motorists have even started gunfights to settle the right of way. A jogger doesn't stand a chance.

Once I was past Sea World, traffic quieted down somewhat. I could afford to turn on my radio headset and tune out the noise around me. There were no cheering fans along the way on this big run, no Boy Scouts passing out orange slices and hard candies. This would be a private achievement if I could keep it up the whole way home. The weather had turned wet and miserable, the scenery was unremarkable, and the pain I felt had leveled off at its same boring intensity. The only thing to do was focus inward and try to entertain myself.

Aaron Copland's *Billy the Kid Suite* came on the radio, sad in parts but of a perfect complexity for keeping me interested during my run. I realized after a few more miles that I had begun chanting to myself, a stupid mnemonic that lulled me into a half dream state and kept me from calculating how far I had to go and debating on whether or not to stop.

"GUTS and TOES, GUTS and TOES, GUTS and TOES," I sang to myself as I ran. The phrase had nothing to do with running, actually, had no relation to form or fortitude. GUTS and TOES were a couple of those goony anagrams my physicist friend Dave occasionally drops on me when he's revising his textbook and needs a layman to explain things to. Last year he tried me out on the mysteries of black holes. This year he outlined the differences between two mathematical models for the universe that go beyond Einstein and attempt to explain the whole enchilada. The Grand Unifying Theory (the GUT) is a little flawed because it doesn't account for gravity. Proponents of the Theory of Everything (TOE), however, go way beyond the four dimensions we know about and speculate that there are seven dimensions that "fold up" somehow and precede those dimensions we can account for.

"It all sounds a little too mystical to be science," I said.

"Listen to *this,* " he said, pulling out a book called *God and the New Physics.* "Physicists are now talking about the 'self-creating universe,' a cosmos that erupts into existence spontaneously, much as a subnuclear particle sometimes pops out of nowhere in certain high-energy processes."

It seemed to me that they were just eliminating the problem with double talk. "You know what dirty Harry always says, Dave. 'Opinions are like assholes. Everybody has one.' "

The tone of our dialogue breaks down a little when I feel I've slipped out of my depth with Dave. It's a sign for him to tighten up his presentation. Still, I liked the idea of all those different dimensions folding in or out on themselves like a chambered nautilus. What would the various chambers defining reality contain? Coincidental other universes paralleling our own, perhaps, in dimension six, all of history fleshed out in its entirety coming around to meet the future like a snake biting its tail in dimension seven? That's a dimension I would gladly seek out in some time machine of the future. Who wouldn't like to go back into the past to revise or just relive his life? I think sometimes of all the years William and I shared before his stroke, the wonderful times that have accumulated and shaped the vessel of our lives' friendship, out there somewhere, intact in the seventh dimension.

How can I say that the William I know and love now, disabled, dependent, sometimes childlike in his perceptions, is any less real than the William who took me to visit Auden for a week in Austria the summer before he died, or the William who met my challenge flat out and admitted in the middle of a party at Bread Loaf that he wanted to go to bed with me? We still get the thumbs up from awestruck teenagers when we drive around in the little '62 Mercedes sportscar he had when we first met. The wit, the self-assurance, the Byzantine intelligence still inform his decisions, "the shape of his mind," as he would say. None of that is lost to me somehow. I enter the chambered nautilus and can hear him talking with Lowell, moderating a panel at the Library of Congress, defending his decision to boycott the White House. I can trace that spirit in a letter he sent when my terrier died and I was far away from home.

Sunday, 3 April, 1977

Dear Richard,

Astra was hit by a motorcycle this morning and killed. She apparently died on impact, and was lying on the road in front of the barn by the time Bob got there, with Lady standing over her. The boy who hit her tried very hard not to: he braked the bike and went over the handlebars and skidded fifty feet till the bike hit one of the guard posts below the driveway. He did a lot of damage to his new motorcycle, and hurt his leg and his hand—I tell you all this because if you'd been here you would have felt, I think, that he did what he could to avoid the accident. I couldn't believe she was dead, because there was hardly a scratch on her, and she didn't make a sound—we were all working near the road, I in the rock garden, Bob and several of the boys digging trees on the slope below the driveway.

It was nobody's fault. The two bikes—there were two friends—weren't speeding, and the boy endangered his life trying to stop and turn. Astra has run on this property for years and years and knew about the road. I suppose she was just running across it.

What can I say. The Dawleys are all stricken. Even K, who is not a great dog lover, cried. She went down to the Point with me, where we buried Astra under the red pine, on the other side from my wonderful poodle Sandy. I am as sad as I can be. She was such a darling friend of a dog—we had had loving words within an hour of her death. She had a good life, and will not have the trouble of old age, and she knew that she was loved. I was trying to tell the Dawleys how, long ago, she was in the pound in Omaha, and I decided that must have been 1970 when you were in graduate school, so she was probably eight, if you got her as a pup. That makes her my age, I guess. Like me. She seemed to find it a happy age. She looked happy, lying there. I talked to her for a while before Bob told me she was dead.

I will call you at York on Saturday night or Sunday morning after your plane arrives. I feel as wretched about this as any of Astra's friends, maybe even including you.

Yours,
William

Time collapses into itself creating something like an eternal present when you consider that a man's life must mean the totality of that life. William, it seems, must undergo the "trouble of old age," and I can no longer count on beautiful acts of friendship like his letter when bad luck comes barreling around the corner on a country road to stun my heart. But these are only points along a line that continues forward and backward, the continuous present of our friendship. We've helped create the world for each other. The course of that friendship might be rocky at times, sometimes even like jogging in the rain on an island made of garbage, but we decided long ago always to try to run through such bad weather for the sake of the race.

Invariably, the landmark you thought you would never reach fades into the distance behind you and you are finally home. You can take a swim and wash away all the breakdown products polluting your blood, or you can try for a few more miles and push your training to the limit. Maybe you drink a Bloody Mary or two and fall back into bed with your friend to sleep the sleep of the dead until it's time for supper the way I did yesterday when I ran around the bay in San Diego.

Just a week to go. I can hardly believe it. I have to keep in mind all the times I thought I wouldn't make it through a run, the mornings I had to force myself to even start a run at all. I have to remember all that effort now as I approach the final week of training and try to shake this cold. The real letdown, the final irony, is that Betty won't be joining me in the marathon when *she* was the one who got me all fired up in the first place. She has to live her life, of course, and I couldn't expect her to give up the short-term consultantship to Tunisia that has come her way. She likes to work at least one job a year to keep her hand in and to keep her contacts fresh. It is a discipline like running. It would be very easy for her not to do any sort of work, I suppose, just hang out in Europe or wherever and play rich divorcée. I respect her decision. But I mustn't let my disappointment keep me from the goal. Ultimately, running the marathon is something you have to do on your own anyway, I guess.

Sweet Barbie sent me a postcard last week that said, "Hey, Marathon Man, how are your quads doing?" I've got my sister's support, at least. Though she runs, so far she hasn't tried a marathon herself. She comes along and cheers her husband on when he does the Marine Marathon in D.C.: "Go George, all right Georgie. Atta boy." Pink sneakers, pink jogging outfit, and pink pom-poms, a real Marabel Morgan. After raising two kids on her own for fifteen years when her first marriage broke up, she found a wonderful guy who saw eye to eye with her, got an annulment and remarried. She wears mink, drives a big car, and makes gourmet pastries. She's had enough liberation to last a lifetime and likes things just fine the way they are. When I called her to say Hi she said, "Of course you have to do this for yourself, but I want you to know how proud I am of you." I would never have believed that at my age a pretty girl rooting for me in some athletic venture could mean a thing to me. I actually felt myself blushing when she spoke.

When William and I go to bed, regardless of the tensions of

the day, my love for him sometimes overwhelms me a little. So vulnerable, so courageous, and, though I hate to admit it sometimes, so childlike with his hair brushed and smelling of toothpaste, organizing his things for the night. Bottle beside the bed, slippers and a glass of water on the nightstand. Handkerchief under the pillow, pat the dog good night. We read a couple of poems and start the new novel Kurt Vonnegut has sent. "With love and respect for the humane and melodic poet William Meredith, and with thanks for his new and selected poems," the author has written on the title page. William interrupts the reading, a question out of his private reveries.

"John," William says, "what's that?"

"You mean why was he crying when we called him?"

"Yes."

"I guess he misses us. He must be going through a lot now with the divorce."

John has become one of William's closest friends from the Adult Day Center. His illness has taken everything from him, and it's very tough going. The three of us go out to dinner and John and William speak to each other in their halting way, without the pressures to follow a difficult conversation, or act "normal." One could be speaking Chinese to the other, it wouldn't matter. Their mutual sympathy transcends verbal communication. I am something like William's child when John is around, lots of bad jokes at my expense between them, one of the few times he can throw his weight around these days. When the waiter brings the check, of course, I must tally it up and pay, and we return to the real world of disability again.

"He's never cried before," I say. "Things must be tough."

"Trouble now," William says.

"Yeah, I guess he has trouble."

"No, me."

This is one of the few times William has ever indicated to me that he is aware of what his future holds. His friends die routinely, sadly. Howard Moss just recently at age sixty-five. The Academy Institute sends death notice postcards regularly, which

I dread showing him. William is aware that John has had a number of strokes.

"Don't you worry, William. I'll always be with you, no matter what. I love you. We have to play very hard. We have to enjoy ourselves while things are okay."

I promise myself again to try to be kinder to William through the day tomorrow, more patient, more willing to go at his turtle speed. We say the "Our Father," which William can almost say in its entirety by himself. Good therapy for us both.

Dr. Brensilver's antibiotics are working by morning. The fall foliage has more than peaked now. The trees' black limbs are beginning to reach through the brilliant colors as the trees strip down in the wind. Three gray cats lie sleeping around the large orange pumpkin we carved and put on the outside table yesterday: William's design, my execution.

The doctor has said if I try to keep to my schedule this Saturday I should be aware of hypoxia. The chest cold may not let me take in enough air to keep going. But one more run before I taper off this week is crucial, I decide, cold or no cold, since I slacked off last week. I'll just have to nurse the cold all next week and hope for the best on marathon day.

I dress in my blue running pants and coat. The ankle braces have become second nature just as Miss Horn predicted. I set out two glasses of water in the mailbox. The neighbor boy comes roaring around the corner in his '56 Chevy, and I flag him down to ask if he'll drop in on William for a visit while I'm out. "Sure," he says, "no problem."

And I'm off. By the second time I come to Ryan's Hill I can barely breathe, but I get over the hill and my wind comes back. I can feel how much more energy it requires than normally, but I finish the 9.6-mile course. If I don't get my energy back by Sunday, there is little hope of running the full marathon. When I come in from my run William is leafing through old speech therapy lessons by himself as though he were able to read or do homework. Kittymaug is asleep on his lap. He looks up and smiles as though he has been very busy, not to worry that I've left him alone. He's happy I'm running, writing again, drinking less. His response is generous, as usual. Today I like to think I've run in spite of my cold for his sake. I try to think how I can make the marathon day fun for him, so he doesn't have to sit it out alone somewhere.

October 24, 1987

Dear Kitty and Paul,

I wasn't able to reach my friend Betty before you left, but she is back now. I'm sorry I didn't call in any case.

The bad news is that Betty has taken a job and leaves for Tunisia on Tuesday—just like Betty, Tunisia on Tuesday. But like Betty too, she's arranged for us all to use her house and has a friend lined up for me to run with who will be staying at the house with us, some guy named Peter Weller, who has just starred in a film called *Robot Cop* or some such. She says he's very nice.

In any case, I hope you are still planning to be my body bagger after the run. If you can't join us, it would be okay since Svetlana would be happy to have William as a guest for the weekend. But I hope you can come.

We will drive down on Friday night to be able to pick up my number and other race paraphernalia on Saturday. If you want to drive with us, we would stay at Betty's Friday night. Otherwise, we would stay with Paul Friday night and then all go out to Betty's on Saturday when you come down. Sunday morning you could drop me and then go to Paul's to watch the event later in the day. I would make my way up to Paul's apartment after the race, since there's no telling how long I'll take.

Last weekend I ran around the bay in San Diego, about 16 miles, and the ankle held up. But this week I'm nursing a bad cold and don't know just how recouped I'll be. I may have to walk the 26.2, but I plan to make it.

Did you know why the race is 26.2 miles long, by the way? We had dinner with a Brit a few weeks ago, who explained that when England decided to revive the classic marathon around the turn of the century, officials carefully measured out the 26 miles that were run in Greece to end just at the palace. King Edward's (?) wife Alexandra (?) decided instead that she wanted the runners to come through a little courtyard in the palace so she could see them. "A few hundred yards more or less won't kill them, now, will they?"

Well, Cheri has come for lunch and I must be off to cook. We're going to take the boat out of the water today and go for a last ride. I hope this letter finds you back from Spain, that we can all play in New York this weekend.

Love from R and W

To run or not to run, that is the question this morning. Now that the ankle is better my cold threatens to keep me from finishing the marathon. If I could just *will* the sore throat and congested chest away. How much should I run now this last week? It's all guesswork. So close now. I'm going to run the New York City Marathon if I have to tow a respirator behind me. But I want to finish well.

Yesterday a former student of William's came for the day, and I decided not to run. Instead, we spent the afternoon on the river where the light and autumn foliage were almost surrealistic. But the air was bitter cold when we got into the middle of the little bay by the coast guard boat house. And I needed to stand in the river a while bailing out the boat before we could begin sailing. We hadn't seen Cheri all summer long, and she loves William so, we couldn't go back to Washington without seeing her. She was up at six baking bread for us. She brought photographs of her summer vacation and talked for hours of her troubles at work, her pets, her family. It was a lovely visit, the standard Meredith fix for another summer. Sometimes you just have to postpone your work, your running, what have you, when friends are in need.

Yesterday's boat trip hasn't helped my cold any, and this morning's mail has brought another six inches of bills to pile on top of the ones that haven't been paid.

Dear Charlotte Marshall calls this morning to tell me there's a special Marathon Guide in yesterday's *New York Times*. She will give it to me when we come to lunch Friday if I haven't seen it. In her eighties now, she is still so tuned in to things, so engaged and conscientious in the details of friendship. For years she and John directed the Rockefeller Conference Center at Lake Como, a distinguished international retreat for writers, statesmen, and scholars. It is like dining with a baroness when we visit her in Wilton. John has died, and she has her own battle with cancer these days. When she thought the illness might affect her voice box so she could no longer call the cat, she trained the cat to come for its supper by blowing a little silver whistle. I think of her as an elite marathoner in the race she is running.

The pictures in the guide are so exciting, it's like taking a double dose of Comtrex cold tablets. Over forty thousand tried to get in, and twenty-two thousand made it; six thousand of these were foreign runners. When Betty sent me the self-addressed stamped envelope and careful instructions on mailing, I never gave my application a second thought. But I guess I *was* a little lucky to get in.

It may not be as grand as building the Great Pyramid, but this is still a big production: 284 gallons of "marathon blue" to paint the center line from the start at the Verrazano Bridge to the finish at Central Park, 37,000 Milky Way bars to revive runners at the finish, 88,000 safety pins to attach numbers, 30 medical units, 7,000 race day volunteers, 1 million paper cups, nearly 500 portable toilets. There will even be 80 psychiatrists on hand to deal with anxiety attacks.

Twenty-two thousand runners will be out there for all sorts of reasons, but every one of them has had to work as hard as or harder than I have these past months. Every one of them will be nervous, will be giving it all his soul has. If you could harness the energy coming off the Verrazano Bridge November 1, you wouldn't have to worry about what OPEC is up to over the next few years.

The *Times* guide points out that "to be a good spectator, you have to be more than just a face in the crowd." Carry a sign, use a person's name, stay around to cheer the many disabled athletes that may be coming in by wheelchair long after the front-runner. In Italian you call out, "coor-AJ-ee-oh," in French, "coor-RAY," in Spanish, "on-da-LAY," and in English, "LOOK-ing good" as the runners come around the course.

And the guide includes a great article on the history of the various neighborhoods we'll be running through, from Bay Ridge, settled by the Dutch in 1636, to "the most celebrated patch of grass in the world," Central Park, completed by Vaux

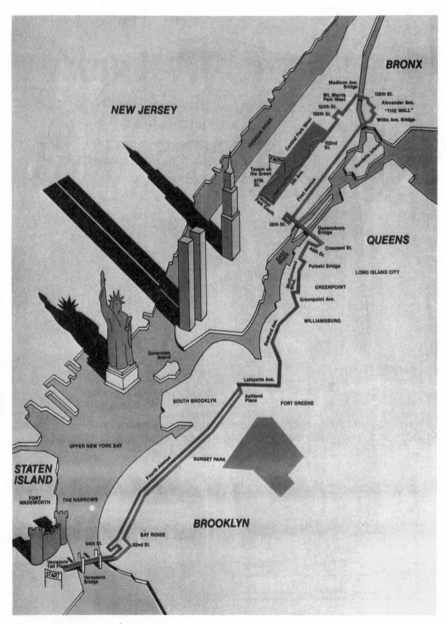

Copyright 1987, New York Road Runners Club.

and Olmsted in 1876. In Brooklyn we run by the offices of the old *Brooklyn Daily Eagle,* which Walt Whitman edited in the 1840s. He'll certainly be there in spirit, "containing" this multitude. We reach the Wall at the Willis Avenue Bridge, then are cheered on through Harlem and down Fifth Avenue for the final five miles home.

Betty says I'm going to make it. I've met just about every challenge in my training along the way, why should this be any different? I can only pray that I will be able to say, as Fred Lebow said after running the 1976 marathon: "I am shocked that it worked."

The goal this week is to train enough to maintain my conditioning and at the same time take it easy enough to try to shake this cold. I've decided on the following schedule for the remainder of the week and am keeping my fingers crossed: Tuesday, one loop (3.2 miles); Wednesday, two loops; Thursday, one loop; Friday, off; Saturday, 2 miles in Central Park; Sunday—RACE DAY.

Once again, this morning's run was harder than it should have been because of my cold. I finished without becoming too winded, but I was *sweating* as though I had run a marathon. Also, William put me through a pretty good workout before I even left bed this morning, and I suppose that siphoned off energy that might have been expended running up Ryan's Hill. It was energy well spent, though.

When I played football in high school there was a lot of locker-room expertise floating around about how sex fit into our training. One coach had a standard lecture that included strict prohibitions on any sort of sexual activity the night before a big game, I recall. The theory was that it weakened the knees, I believe. Actually, I think he just liked watching us squirm as a stony silence fell and he surveyed the room for any degenerates who might be toying with the idea of toying with themselves the night before the match. You could feel the hair begin to grow on your palms in that silence, the prospect of madness entered your consciousness like a cloud drifting over the full moon.

Once a young guy about twenty-three came to my office with classic symptoms of gonorrhea. He was a an Italian-American working in construction and was about as beautiful a specimen of a young man as you could find. I kept my examination very professional, however—gay health practitioners must maintain an objective distance from male patients just the way a straight male doctor must with beautiful female patients. Even though it was a legitimate part of the medical history—too much activity might produce nonspecific urethritis—I must say I took a rather

keen interest when I asked this young man how often he mastur-
bated. I wasn't much older than he was at the time, but his
answer surprised me. He blinked those wonderful black
eyelashes, about a half inch long, and said, "Every day." The
tone of his voice seemed to ask, "Doesn't everybody?"

I imagined him just a few hours earlier tossing in his bed, half
asleep still, taking hold of himself and working off the tensions
built up during his dreams the night before. I asked him to get
dressed and concentrated on changing the train of my thought
to keep from getting aroused myself.

The Protestant kids always had it a lot easier in this regard
when I was growing up. From prepuberty on, it was drilled into
us Catholic kids that sins of self-abuse were mortal, and we went
around half the time sure we would burn for eternity if a truck
happened to hit the school bus. The minister's kids up the street,
though, were simply told not to let masturbation get out of
hand, as it were, and that was it. No cold showers and weekly
vows never to do it again, with six days of guilt until one confessed that one had done it again. The minister's kids horsed
around a while, and then went out to play baseball or deliver
their papers. If someone had only told me it wasn't a big deal
during those difficult private years of adolescence, what a lot of
grief they'd have spared me. I tried to hint as much to my
nephew once without embarrassing him. He is also my godson,
and I think it wasn't out of line. How did St. Francis say it? "Be
kind to your Brother Body."

Sometimes when I'm half dressed before my run, just my
shorts, maybe, and a gym sock, and William's eyes fill with a
certain kind of attention, then I have to tumble back into bed
and forget running. That's about as much as my boyhood neu-
roses will permit me to say on the subject, except perhaps that
our pleasure, happily, remains mutual in such situations.

Once in a while when I am out on the road I will come across
a young housewife who is also jogging, and I have daydreams of
our falling off into the bushes, ripping the clothes from our
sweaty bodies, and going at it. There's something about the
clothes in jogging that's erotic for me. I think of William's lines,

> In a fantasy, Yeats saw himself appear
> to Maud Gonne as a swan,
> his plumage fanning his desire.

I can tell from the way these housewives' eyes drift down below my waist sometimes that they are thinking the same thing as I. Occasionally, the bus filled with old ladies on their way to the senior center will honk at me as I jog, and a few catcalls will trail after me as it zooms up the hill.

Once for a week I ran by a young matron who lingered by her mailbox dressed in a warm-up suit. I could see her sift through the few pieces of mail a mile before I came to her house. I'd have had to be blind not to get her meaning. Her two kids played in the driveway. The housework was all done, no doubt. It was mid-morning, no husband in sight till supper time. I thought of Zorba's notion that it is a mortal sin not to go to bed with a woman who has invited you. But I've made this unneighborly mistake before and have come to learn that such affairs are anything but harmless. Besides, my guilt complex has all it can do to handle occasional philandering with members of my own sex. Most folks feel that bisexuality is a myth, that being part gay is like being part pregnant. In forty years I still haven't figured it out, have given in to my desire for beautiful men and women both when that desire becomes overwhelming.

I think of all the secret love poems William wrote me those years when we had to live in different cities. Though William never demanded "monogamy" in our friendship, it was hard to think of catting around when I got such a letter in the mail.

POEM

> The swans on the river, a great
> flotilla in the afternoon sun
> in October again.
>
> In a fantasy, Yeats saw himself appear
> to Maud Gonne as a swan,
> his plumage fanning his desire.

One October at Coole Park
he counted fifty-nine wild swans.
He flushed them into a legend.

Lover by lover is how he said they flew,
but one of them must have been without a mate.
Why did he not observe that?

We talk about Zeus and Leda and Yeats
as if they were real people, we identify constellations
as if they were drawn there on the night.

Cygnus and Castor & Pollux
are only ways of looking at
scatterings of starry matter,

a god putting on swan-flesh
to enter a mortal girl
is only a way of looking at love-trouble.

The violence and calm of these big fowl!
When I am not with you
I am always the fifty-ninth.

Today the calendar says it's Alan Bradford's turn to come read with William. Each of the friends who visits to practice speech has developed his own system of working with William. Alan likes to chat about goings-on at the English department where they taught together. Louise Ames tries to put William's phrases into sentences and then transcribes the sentences for study: "I am fixing up the world. I see it, then do not see it. It is difficult and frustrating. Sometimes I am lucid, at other times not. The inscription reads: To Julia Randall, with love, William. I know Julia for ten years. Julia lives alone, fifty miles outside Baltimore. We're colleagues. Julia is crotchety, but nice. Sometimes I am crotchety also. We heard Canada geese honking and crows cawing from the top of the spruce. For thirty years I've tolerated engine noises across the river."

My favorite language activity with William is simply to read to him. When we go to bed this night I continue the new Kurt

Vonnegut novel, but my throat is too sore to read much. I ask William if he is getting my cold. "Are you feeling hot?" I ask him. "Nope," he says in one of the surprising phrases that sometimes just pop out, "cold as a clam." Tomorrow I decide I will take him to the barber. I mustn't get too preoccupied with this journal, or the bills, or running. His health is good now, he's funny and alert and doing his best to support me in this running project. We have to live every day to its fullest.

Cancellations are covered in the small print on the fact sheet they send you once your application for the marathon has been approved. If you plan to drop out at the last minute, they want to be sure someone else on the waiting list has a chance to run. I read about how to cancel as though I were looking down from a very high bridge, feeling that deep subliminal curiosity about jumping.

This evening Mother calls from Florida to wish me luck. Even the Florida papers are filled with news about marathon weekend, and she's worried about the prediction of hot weather. I'm coming down to the wire now. It is exhilarating but scary too. What will happen to me at the Wall? They make it very convenient to drop out safely at any point in the run.

"If you experience any injury or discomfort, stop at the next medical aid station," the brochure informs you. This morning I couldn't even finish one loop without beginning to limp, and the best I can hope for, I think, is to be able to ignore the pain enough to get through. Yesterday I ran two loops without too much difficulty by taking Advil before running, to cut down the inflammation. Problem was that I also cut down the pain, and I probably wouldn't have run as far yesterday if I had felt the ankle getting worse. This evening there I was again, whirlpool and ultrasound at the Connecticut College training room trying to stimulate healing. I guess I've decided not to try anything else now until the morning of the run, give it the best possible chance to repair a little. I can only hope the limping won't start until well into the race and that I can take the pain till I finish. Maybe it won't be so bad, though, who knows?

My "free" time today has been spent on the details of getting to New York and arranging to have William join me. He could stay in Connecticut, but it's going to be a lot of fun and I want him to share that. Before Betty left she gave me the name of some friends who will help us, and gave me a few last-minute tips about the race. I'm supposed to wear my oldest warm-up suit because when the race begins, everyone strips down to running shorts and throws his sweats on a big pile, which are salvaged and given away. If I stay at Betty's I won't have to catch the bus from race headquarters at the Sheraton at six in the morning, a very important saving of sleep hours. Some friends from her racing club are throwing a pasta party the night before the marathon, and I'm invited. The idea is to load up on carbohydrates before the race to have the energy to carry you through. And they will take me to the Fort Wadsworth staging area on Staten Island Sunday morning.

Kitty and Paul have returned from Spain, but have run into a disaster that will keep them from joining me and William in New York. I think I can have William stay with the Enders Saturday night. If I find a parking space on Friday, I don't plan to move the car until we head for home. New York is bound to be the world's biggest traffic jam for the entire weekend. The day after the marathon we are to have dinner in New London with Martha, and I sure hope nothing will keep me from driving. The next day I'm supposed to drive to New Haven for a cystoscopy to see if the old bladder cancer has returned. Next Friday we go to Los Angeles for the *Los Angeles Times* Book Award and visit friends in San Francisco. Then a Literary Lions dinner at the New York Public Library, and two days later we pack up our household and head for Washington. I guess I really do try to put too much into too little time. If the day is empty in the calendar, I tend to just fill it in without any consideration of how things are building. I've got to work on that for both our sakes. After the holidays I don't plan to move for weeks.

Philip called this morning. He has decided to run the marathon, but at this late date he's been put on a waiting list. He keeps calling to see if I still plan to run. I expected him to make the pitch to use my number if I didn't run. Instead he gave me the good news that he had been accepted for the race and would be joining me. I guess maybe I inspired him to apply after our visit this summer. Wonderful.

Philip plans to run the race in about three hours and forty minutes, at least an hour or so faster than I will do, no doubt. But that's okay if he really does do that well. The beauty of this event is that you actually are competing against yourself. Philip will be in the blue starting area, which includes the men with numbers 1–15,999. The red start includes women and first-time male runners who don't plan to run particularly fast. The two groups run on different sides of the bridge and don't join up for the first seven miles or so of the race. Dr. Brensilver is hooked on jogging too and has run the New York City Marathon several times. He tells me the red starting lane has the advantage, since it is likely to be less congested and I can kick ahead. *He* can kick ahead, rather. Every time he calls he asks me what I expect my finishing time to be. I tell him the ladies and I will do just fine chugging over the Verrazano Bridge, taking in the scenery.

Norm has come in while I sit typing in an adjacent room during William's sculpture class to say, "I've got to hand it to William, he sure keeps at it when he falls down." And, of course, William has fallen again. In the men's room his left forearm is bloody, and he is starting to get black and blue. He doesn't seem to have hit his head, though. With the anticoagulant medication he takes, the big danger is hemorrhage. We might not be able to stop bleeding in the brain. It is time to go home. Nothing seems broken. William is sheepish and apologetic. He is so intense about his sculpting that he will sit for hours without a break, so that when he gets up his balance is gone.

I make a fire in the Jotul woodstove, call Anthony to see if William can stay with them on Saturday night, and apply an ice pack to William's arm. In front of the flames of the open stove we relax finally. It has been a big day for us both. During one of Louise's visits she has left me a note in her lessons, which says:

Dear Richard,
    William and I agree that each morning William should eat his cereal and be dressed for walking by ten, rain or shine. Ann will tour the garden and arboretum with William at ten, then speak and read with him for the next hour, on the porch or sofa. After this daily session William will review the writing while Ann washes the dishes. William feeds the one tan kitten and the dog.

So this morning we tried to be up by nine at William's insistence. Only trouble was that all night long William was up with the obsession that a door was open in the house. He kept insisting that I check the door of the refrigerator, and neither of us slept at all. I tried to explain to Louise once that William's seizures were a result of sleep deprivation and that I had long ago decided that William was to sleep as late as he wished. The seizures are awful for him and can be life-threatening. Like running a marathon, actually—the body freezes up finally from all the neurons firing at once—and his heart is significantly compromised already. We sleep late, baby ourselves if you wish, thank you very much.

On the other hand, Louise is one of the really loyal friends here. She comes back rain or shine in spite of her own very busy schedule. So I shouldn't mind her puritan notion of rising early. I'm sure she thinks that I'm just fond of lying abed or that I dally over the mail while I keep William from the full fruits of a day's labor. Louise is one of the sweet people who insist that there must be some way of pulling the poems out of William that are surely *there*. And I know I must never give up either, though people like Louise don't quite understand that writing a poem is a living process, something like a dance, where you experiment with thought and language and sound, in and out, back and forth, that poems are alive when they are growing into shape. Louise considers them something like chiseled tablets of the soul that one needs only to make a rubbing of for posterity. But she keeps at it and she is probably right. Today her notes contain the following attempt:

"From the hilltop, Ann and William had a long view of the river."

> Fall Leaves:
> Brown oak,
> Green beech,
> Yellow beech, Underneath
> the hemlock
> bough, we see the
> leaves of Autumn.

This really isn't too bad, has a kind of oriental simplicity. At least Louise is working at what she wishes to see in William, a return to language and poetry. And each person, each real friend of William, tries to do the best for him the way he or she sees fit. It is quite beautiful, if a little annoying at times. "Now you will get up at nine." Louise has four children who have just about left the nest. There is a certain mother mode that is in part the source of her genius, and I guess she's feeling the empty nest a little.

Before I go to bed I must remind myself not to forget all the hours of running, the hot days, the pain, the effort to train for this marathon. In spite of the weak ankle and recuperation from a bad cold, I owe myself the best rousing finish that I can give to this project. I mustn't use these illnesses as an excuse. I have already done something significant in trimming maybe fifteen to twenty pounds off this frame. At least I *look* that much trimmer. And it will be worth it to do something hard now this weekend. One article in the *Times* guide said that once a runner dedicated this run to a dead brother. This will be dedicated to a living brother—dear William—and me too. I'm going to run for pride in our friendship, like some young Greek marathoner might have done thousands of years ago for his lover.

Well, tomorrow is the big day. I sure wish I'd thought to have Philip or Betty or someone else pick up my number for me. I'm sitting on the edge of a tree planter at the corner of 53rd and Avenue of the Americas, only one-half block into the line that winds around the corner and disappears down the street. A cheeky pedestrian coming the other way has just informed us we're only ninety minutes away from the front door of the hotel lobby where we register. The weather is what I would call brisk, but the guy behind me holding my place in line as we snake along says that this is still too hot to run a marathon. He's run it before and should know. I think it's damn cool and that my cold will progress to pneumonia as I sit here on this cement planter. My butt is already getting a little numb as the cold seeps in.

Charlotte was so sweet when we stopped in Wilton on the way to New York yesterday. I hope I'm that sharp and dignified when I'm eighty-one. Wonderful lunch out of her husband's cookbook: coq au vin (Madeira), asparagus with Parmesan cheese, and rice pudding with raspberries, which she heaped on top of the pudding for me. "You must be pleased to be able to eat all you wish now, Richard," she said. She'd read the *Times* Marathon Guide in last Sunday's paper and was well informed as usual.

I think Charlotte has finally accepted that I might be okay, that William might be lucky to have me around. Her judgments were always a little severe in the old days when I felt I had to speak my "hippie" mind, and "Tell it like it is" was the rule of the day.

One of the things Charlotte was most proud of when John was alive was his membership in a men's club in New York called the Century Association. It includes artists, college presidents, foundation and museum directors, and various celebrities. A New Yorker cartoon I saw once characterizes it perfectly. One very old man in an overstuffed armchair smiles at another very old man and says, "Stuffy in here, isn't it?"

William is a member, and I thought it would be fun to be able to join him at member's meetings and be stopped at the door because I looked too *young* to be a member. Four years ago Joe Parriot put me up and solicited the additional letters of recommendation required.

Charlotte promised to join us for the new members' celebration when I got in, but I'm sure she never thought it was a promise she'd have to keep. At lunch I was pleased to inform her that they had finally deigned to admit me. This put me over the hump as far as her approval rating went.

I suppose I ought to be in line now taking in the excitement with other runners waiting to get in to pick up their registration packets. Betty insists that I have to meet more people my own age, and I have nothing against that. It's become hard for me to reach out to people these past years, sharing the relative immobility and silence of William's world the way I do. Today, though, there's a kind of psychic contagion in the air that's pretty irresistible. The smell of hot dogs and soft pretzels comes wafting over here every few seconds. All sorts of hawkers are trying to interest runners in bronzed running shoes on a plaque, discount coupons on items at various sports stores, even old issues of *USA Today* that describe marathon madness. One flier offers 15 percent off its merchandise and explains,

We're not in the missionary business. We're in the athletic gear business. So, what we hope is a whole herd of runners will invade our store and buy us out. So, what we give up in profit margin, we make up in volume. This is the New York way. Beat the competition to death. Now, you say, what kind of junk are you going to try to unload on us poor runners? Well, this isn't junk. This is top of the line, name brand stuff. This stuff will knock your eyeballs out. We have shoes. We have clothes. And being immodest, our store is a blockbuster. So, you better check us out. And you could, if you want, throw all those other flyers from the other stores away. In the trash cans, please. We gotta try to keep this town semi-clean.

Just now a red-haired fellow with an Irish accent comes over to me to see what it is I am reading and says, "Hey fellow, what do you know that's good?"

"Not the weather, for sure. I'm trying to beat a cold, and I've had enough vitamin C to ward off the plague."

When we finally got into town last night William and I had a nap and then set out to find an Italian restaurant to get down some more pasta. The taxi driver gave us a recommendation, though he explained that it is against the law to give such tips. The more carbohydrates I've eaten this week, the greater my need for *good* carbohydrates has become. Louis Jr.'s was the best place in town according to him, on 53rd between Second and Third. Louis Jr. in the flesh turned out to be an eighty-year-old Italian gentleman the color of week-old spaghetti who stood greeting customers as they came in the door. The first thing he asked was if I planned to run in the marathon.

"As a matter of fact, yes," I said, thinking it might mean a free plate of ravioli. This is New York, however, and all it meant was a wish for success in my run, which is better than a poke in the eye with a sharp stick, as William used to say. Sometimes William is so charming people make such offers out of the blue. But the pasta was "real Italian," well worth seeking out, with spumoni and espresso coffee afterward. Then home for a fitful sleep—working out in my dreams how I would quit school and live with William, deciding that he wouldn't have many more years and that I should spend those years with him and not just commute on weekends. I was happy when I woke up and found that it was true.

It's getting colder as I sit here in this wind tunnel beside a skyscraper. it's a marathon effort just to get registered. I'll have a fever by morning. Why didn't I bring a scarf?

I've met a sweet, corn-fed girl named Angie and her boyfriend Jim while standing on line. She's let me type sitting on the bench a hundred yards ahead, and calls me in as the line catches up to me. "Keep writing," she says in very serious tones when we finally get to the entrance and are fed into the yellow plastic chains that mark off chutes for entrants in the main ballroom.

Angie is a sports journalist herself and is very happy about my project to document my training. My biggest goal, I explain to her, is to run the entire distance even if it takes the whole day, so I can say I *ran* the marathon. Betty has always said I should simply walk if I'm injured. Marathoners are obsessive about the sport, but they aren't crazy. Part of the game is knowing just how far to push yourself and still enjoy the training safely. The best runners are the most gentle on this subject, are the least competitive. Everyone forgives someone *else* for walking during the marathon, but tries not to accept it for himself.

At the first station in line we presented our computerized acceptance form and were given a bib number with several pull-off tickets enabling us to eat at the pasta party at Tavern on the Green, go to the disco party Sunday night, keep a small bag on the buses with a change of dry clothes after the race, and, if we paid our five dollars, take a bus from the New York Public Library out to the starting line. The buses were to begin leaving at the ungodly hour of six, and I couldn't imagine running a race if I got up early enough to catch one. Thank God for Betty's invitation to stay out at her house on Staten Island the night before the race, even though she was off in Tunisia.

The next station fitted you out with complimentary running shorts advertising Perrier, a T-shirt praising Manufacturers Hanover, and a cap with a Mercedes logo on the visor beautifully made up. For a twenty-dollar entry fee, the Road Runners Club was doing a nice job with freebies and doing okay by the sponsors as well. The gift pack included a full tube of skin cream designed for outdoor athletes, and even provided enough safety pins to attach your number to your shirt and a claim check for your bag. A shopping bag full of printed material announced everything from the route of the course to starting times for marathons from Budapest to Malaysia.

Publications ran articles on how clean and sweet a runner's sweat is, a veritable sexual stimulant for both sexes. One described what a social experience training with friends can be. Another described the danger of running when it has begun to feel like an obligation. The whole point of the training is to enjoy the run and make it standing up. The magazine offered all sorts of tips from toilet training (keep your eyes open for signs marking the spot when you first feel the urge to stop) and dressing for the weather to proper pacing (save your energy for the finish). The information package included hundreds of details from where to catch the bus to what restaurants were featuring high-carbohydrate specials.

At the end of the registration line runners came into a room called the "gift shop." This concession was hardly the little specialty store implied by the name, however. Perhaps a thousand runners crowded three-deep at tables laden with marathon memorabilia. I debated a long time between two different pouches to strap around my waist while running, trying each on and jogging in place to see how it felt. I finally decided on the slightly larger one, a red quarter moon slung at the small of the back and kept in place with Velcro tabs in the front. It weighed nothing but was large enough to carry Band-Aids, a chocolate bar, Vaseline, Ben Gay, chewing gum, money, and ID card in case you passed out or got hit by a car, a plastic canteen, and anything else you might wish to bring along.

Two young guys, maybe twenty-eight, stood beside me buying out the store. They tried on the various beanies with little visors that joggers and European cyclists preferred, selected one of the coffee mugs they didn't already own, and pulled on designer sweaters with stick men jogging across a big apple on the chest. In their matching sweaters they were like twins in a toothpaste commercial, except that one was blond and the other had thick black hair. Trim, with brilliant smiles, they spoke to each other with enough affection to be lovers. Heartbreaking.

"Where you from?" I asked. I couldn't resist them.

"Toronto," the blond boy said, and smiled at me eagerly. I could feel myself blushing.

It was the first marathon for them too, but this, of course, wasn't just *any* marathon. It was the New York City Marathon, and these guys were as wide-eyed as kids on a shopping spree at F.A.O. Schwarz the week before Christmas. The Boston might be more exclusive, the Beijing more exotic, and the Marine more strictly American, but everyone agreed that New York City was the mega-marathon, the World Series of running, and these two young Canadians couldn't get enough of the prerace electricity, the city, the people.

When our orders were filled we all wished one another the best of luck and said goodbye. It was enough just to shake their hands and smile back into those beautiful open faces, one more infusion of the good will and excitement that was building in me like the rising tension in a bridegroom who has kept celibate for weeks before his wedding night.

As we endured the ordeal of getting through registration an esprit de corps began to develop that foreshadowed tomorrow's race. Folks struck up a conversation without any sense of compunction the way they might while waiting on line in a grocery store before a hurricane or a big snowstorm hit town. A single thought was running through everyone's mind: "Look out, man, here it comes." A little masochistic, maybe, but people seem to relish the anticipation of running 26.2 miles, so they can pump up enough adrenalin to cope with the pain that is coming down the road.

When I came out of the congested hotel lobby a man who looked seventy-five began grousing good-naturedly, "It almost took longer to get through the line than to run the race."

"What time are you looking for?" I asked.

"Last year I finished in four hours thirty," he said. In spite of the flappy jowls and balding head, it was clear he wasn't kidding and expected me to be duly impressed. I thought of my own training all summer long and imagined going through that at age seventy-five, and was duly impressed. "But I think I'll do a little better this year," he said. "How about you?"

"I just want to finish the whole course without stopping," I said.

"How far have you run?"

"Well, a couple of weeks ago I did seventeen miles," I said. "And I've tried to do thirty to forty miles a week. But I've been nursing a bum ankle, and I have this sickening feeling that I might have to walk the last ten miles, or hobble in on one leg."

"You'll be okay," he said. "If you have to walk, just walk. No need to cripple yourself. But if you've been training like that, you should be just fine."

"I hope so, and I hope you break four-thirty," I said. My turn in line for a taxi had come up, and I waved back to him as I headed for Paul's apartment on the Upper East Side where we were staying. Since Kay's death last year, William's brother-in-law has welcomed us at their old apartment anytime we're in town, a chance to ward off his loneliness and keep her memory alive through her brother. But he understood my wish to spend race night at Betty's house, for my sake and William's.

When I got back to the apartment William had dutifully packed our bags for the trip to Staten Island. He reluctantly agreed to have lunch before we headed out. Eating in restaurants is one of the few things we fight about these days, really. The stroke knocked out most of his taste buds—"Taste buds closed," he explains to friends sometimes, as though they were tiny roses gone to sleep in the night. Eating is something William does more from necessity than pleasure now, and he can't see any point in paying New York prices for food he can't appreciate.

Old "skinflint" William is perfectly prepared to pay thousands for an antique chair he happens to like, or finance a deserving student's education, but he can't abide having a little Wiener schnitzel at the Movenpik when we can fry it up at home for a fraction of the price. Of course, it's always up to Richard to get out in that kitchen and rattle those pots and pans. The day before the marathon I just wanted to treat myself and savor the sights and smells and sounds of the pep rally New York was throwing for eleven million people.

William wore the marathon beanie I placed on his head and dutifully ate his borscht while I wolfed down the Marathon Lasagna featured as the daily special.

"You know, honey, I want you to know how grateful I am for all your sacrifices this summer. I feel as though I've deserted you.

But next week when we go to California we're going to do whatever you like. We're going to do exercises and speech therapy every day, no matter what."

"Good."

"And we're going to play and soak up all the awards and honors they give you, and I'm going to be very proud of the big cheeseburger I got hooked up with."

"I love you."

"Oh, I love you too, William. So much. I'm so grateful for our friendship."

I like to believe that William always understands everything when I talk with him, that he follows the movie we happen to be watching, or the newscast. I know that even if he does get all the words, sometimes the meaning of what he understands gets obscured or colored, as though he were trapped under ice and watching rescuers' broad gestures from above. For some months after he first came back from the hospital I had to be very careful about what play we might go to, what television show we watched. Once, at the Arena Theater, we had to leave when a powerful scene involving an African devil dance scared him. He knew it was only a play, but it was like those moments when you've just awakened from a nightmare and are gripped by a residual terror just the same. This summer's little obsession with the crow that made off with the kitten had him telling anyone who came into the house how a "crow got him," the way you might say a neighbor's house burned down or a friend has died suddenly of a heart attack. Still, the crow *was* a little sinister and had me a little spooked too. William's imaginative and emotional life has always been about as complex as any interior garden I've ever had the chance to glimpse into. It accounts for the originality of his gift, the Byzantine shape of his mind. It's only the *expression* of that rich life that is blunted, appearing simple at times.

When we came up from the basement restaurant we nearly ran into a man whose face was split down the middle, covering him with blood and gore. He was walking with a woman whose skin was green and wart-infested under her tall pointy black hat. Not unusual for New York, you might say, and it took me a moment to realize that we were about to get caught up in the annual Halloween parade if we didn't catch a taxi fast and get to the Staten Island ferry.

Our cab crawled through the traffic as we headed downtown and gave us a chance to inspect the crowd at each stoplight. The darker it got the more people came out in force—standard vampires and ghosts and goblins, yes, but also walking televisions, six men in an earwig outfit, and even a fire-spewing Godzilla. It was going to be a full-moon night in New York, but we had agreed to join Betty's running club for a final plate of pasta, and I had promised myself I'd be in bed by ten.

The ferry pulled out like a floating island loaded with tired refugees from the craziness of Manhattan. It was getting darker earlier these days, and soon daylight saving time would steal even more life from the tailend of the day. Like field mice after the cornstalks are stripped, people would begin to move indoors to live their winter lives. Half of the sun swam on the horizon, a brilliant orange hemisphere, improbable as a stage set, throwing the Statue of Liberty into black relief. People dozed, no one spoke, the babies seemed content to take a breather with the rocking of the ferry. Only a few shutterbug tourists clicked away at Ms. Liberty with their little pocket Kodaks. In a week they will get back fifteen pitch-black photographs with a tiny dot of orange light just barely visible in the center.

"Follow the signs for the trains," our host said on the phone, "and my son Bobby will meet you. You can't miss him. He's got, uh, long hair."

At the top of the stairs stood a young man who only needed satin breeches and high-heeled pumps to pass for Louis XIV, except it was no Halloween getup. He was like a cocoa poodle who had overdosed on Helsinki Formula. The hair fell in perfect chocolate ringlets almost to the small of his back.

"Mista Meredith," he said. "I'm Bobby. My fawtha asked me to pick ya up."

One of the Little Charity nuns who taught us in high school

came from Staten Island and was always saying things like, "Bahwy, keep yaw thawts to yaself," when we laid our witticisms on the assembled algebra class. It was like studying math in a foreign language. I also took a little Spanish in sophomore year, so I can make out okay reading a menu when I'm in Italy or Portugal. Even with this preparation, though, Staten Islandese remains a real challenge.

"Hi, Bobby. Glad to meet you," I said. "I'm Richard. Gee, it was really good of you to pick us up."

"Awe, no prahblem," he said, flashing a big smile. He picked up our luggage, poured us into a little Japanese car, and loaded the tape deck with a U2 cassette.

"So, Richard, ya running tomorrah, or what?" he shouted over the music.

"I guess so," I shouted back.

William poked me in the shoulder blades, and when I turned around he gestured that his ears were exploding.

"Say Bobby, would you mind lowering the music a little? The speakers are blasting out my bud, back there."

"Awe, no prahblem," Bobby said, flashing a big smile. "So Richard, ya ready for the wall?" he asked.

"The wall?"

"Yeah, my fawtha says around twenty miles ya staht having second thawts."

"Oh that. Yeah. I try not to think about it. Like Alzheimer's."

"Aw *right.* "

Bobby looked into his rearview mirror and administered one of his smiles. He moved his seat forward to give William a little more leg room.

"Do you run, Bobby?" I asked.

"Naw, I play in a rock band," he said. I didn't immediately see how the one precludes the other, but he did seem dedicated to music. He was in his sophomore year at the local community college, majoring in guitar, though he explained he would have to learn a lot of other instruments if he hoped for a music degree.

"I really like your hair," I said.

"Thanks," he said, tossing his head a little to shake his locks.

"A lot of people think it means you're a hippie or a bum or something. But I don't bother with them. You still can have long hair and be an okay guy."

He finished every sentence with that shy smile. He was very sweet.

"Say, Bobby, would you mind if I felt your hair?"

"No prahblem," he said. "People ask me that all the time."

One Sunday at church when I was about six years old the head of the lady in the pew in front of me rose majestically through a triangle of three cinnamon minks. Their tiny feet and amber eyes were preserved with a taxidermist's care. Each little mink was biting the butt of the mink in front of him as they ran over the lady's shoulders. By the time the ushers came around for the collection I couldn't stand it anymore and reached out to touch the creatures. When Mother looked up from her missalette I had just begun to stroke their satin fur. She reached out to pull my hand away, and I grabbed on more tightly. We proceeded to choke the lady in her own fur noose with this little tug-of-war and managed to spill the collection basket all over the floor. The lady in the fur was indignant, but grateful for the attention.

Bobby's hair had the same hypnotic power over me. It wasn't a sexual thing, at least not consciously. But I was itching to get a handful of that hair just to feel what it was like. And, indeed, it was smooth and shiny and buoyant like an angel's. I imagined those curls tumbling over his naked shoulders and realized it was time to take my hand away. Bobby said he'd drop us off at Betty's and come back later to take us to the party after he stopped by to *see his girlfriend.*

Oh, the wonders of sex. How do people ever get together, go from meeting each other in the subway to wrapping themselves around each other for the purpose of giving and taking pleasure? Every single sexual encounter in my life has been something like a little miracle for me. And it seems as though twice as much social skill is required to consummate such a tango when two *men* are involved.

Make your best pitch to some young lady you find attractive, and the most you probably risk is a curt "Thanks, but no thanks." Still, you gave it the old college try, and all the world loves a lover.

Try to get some nice young guy to horse around with you on a summer evening, and if you're not careful you may wind up with a punch in the nose or a visit to your local jail. "Making a complicated matter more complicated," William says, in one of his poems on the subject. What right-thinking person would *choose* the extra hassle of living his life as a sexual outlaw if one's emotional life was merely a matter of choice?

Like most guys of his generation, Bobby seemed to consider being gay just another "life-style," like deciding whether to wear earrings or a green Mohawk haircut. He had his generation's sophistication, however, for making it quite clear on which side of the fence *he* stood. After he helped us unload our bags at Betty's he gave us a firm hand, the famous smile, and was off at concert hall decibels to pay his respects to the Juliet in question.

For an hour or two we knocked around Betty's house unpacking our bags and getting ready for dinner. I did a little check to get the hot water and furnace working and make sure no one had robbed her while she was away. The Dali paintings were all intact, sunflowers turning into fried eggs, nymphs playing along the seashore. A flock of grade B Spanish film stars radiated from photos covering the kitchen walls, long, loving inscriptions scrawled over their protuberant bosoms. Fresh towels had been laid out for us, the fridge was filled with staples peculiar to our taste, right down to the diet tonic water. On top of the *New York Times* Marathon Guide Betty had set out four safety pins to attach my bib number to my shirt. She had even put out a fancy pink hat with a note asking me to wear it and think of her during the race, like carrying the queen's hanky during the joust. But it was strange, a little sad even, to be in her house when she was off in Africa.

Betty's running club all thought she was something special too, but they didn't know anything about the glamorous side of her life. They only knew her as a good neighbor who took an interest in people's problems and traveled a lot. The club members were all just folks from the island, a policeman's wife, a real estate broker, a high school coach. One had a severely retarded son, one had just been elected to the town council. Everyone had his story to tell. She didn't need to pretend she was any better than anyone else.

Fifteen of us crowded around a dining room table designed for eight, passing around plates of salad, ziti, and garlic bread, everyone talking at twice the level one would use at Yankee Stadium.

Betty had snitched on us, and both the men and women outdid themselves filling our plates and looking after us. Half the people walking around lower Manhattan claim to be poets, but in some ways Staten Island is as far away from SoHo as Sioux Falls. Our hosts couldn't get enough of the rara avis that had landed in their dining room. So many eager faces turned in our direction when we spoke, I thought they might expect us literally to sing for our supper or ask for the butter in rhymed couplets.

One woman, a beauty, the spitting image of Anne Bancroft, kept jumping up and intercepting our plates as they got passed down the line so she could hand them to us herself. *Runner's World* had published a picture of her crossing the finish line last year with a Cover Girl smile and pink T-shirt that read "Amazing Grace." She certainly was.

Grace took it on herself to introduce us to all the other dinner guests and fill us in on all the details of who was running, who was the official photographer, who wasn't running and why. (Her husband had pulled a muscle, and so rather than run he would deliver us at the start, take William to his brother-in-law's to watch the race, then collect us at the finish line.) A girlfriend of one of the runners would act as the photographer this year.

Not everyone was "high" on the marathon, however. As we cleaned up in the kitchen one guest admitted that she never planned to run a marathon again. She was *not* extolling the rush of crossing the finish line, the beautiful energy of thousands of runners at the start. In the middle of the race last year she had had to give up the race. She was still very disappointed, even bitter, about not meeting her expectations. Sadly, she seemed to consider it a kind of failure. She didn't want to bring me down, but that's the way it had happened for her, she said.

Perhaps the oldest runner in the group was close to fifty, graying hair, dark eyes, soft-spoken. He seemed like the group's rabbi; he kept telling me to *enjoy* the race. Joy seemed to be the name of the game. The ones who had already run a marathon all agreed. The room was pretty electric with nervous energy, but this nervousness was all part of the joy of running, our rabbi explained, quoting his favorite marathon guru. The older we get, the more we understand play, the more we can appreciate the joy of setting up challenges and succeeding.

The only guy at dinner who didn't seem to have a date and who pulled on a bottle of Pabst Blue Ribbon throughout the night said he was sitting out the race this year because he was just too lazy at the end of the summer to train. He would "challenge" himself *next* year.

He was balding a little prematurely and his eyesight might not be so hot, but everything else about him was a knockout. Last summer he had ridden his bicycle cross-country, coast-to-coast, with Grace's teenage son, and from his waist down he looked like Baryshnikov in blue jeans. He even had the dancer's same blue eyes and deep dimples when he smiled. As we were being introduced someone's husband threw his arm over the guy's shoulder and said, "I'm with *him*," in that clumsy way a blue-collar worker teases a man who is a little too beautiful. And the crimson blush the remark produced only made the problem worse, of course. Was this sweet guy blushing for our sake, did he get the picture with me and William and feel his friend was being rude? Clearly he wasn't gay himself but had that kind of sensibility you hope for in straight people when things get a little dicey socially.

Grace teased him like an older sister about the number of times he had given a false osprey alert or eagle sighting as they ran through the bird sanctuary when what they were really looking at was only a large black crow or a sea gull. Everyone loved him, clearly, but there was some distance that kept him from the natural ease the other members of this little running family shared with one another. He seemed special or shy like James

Dean in *Rebel Without a Cause*. Social reality was too complex somehow, like living life with the fractured vision of a cubist painting.

All night he spoke to me with such kindness, like a brother, giving me tips about holding back in the race so I wouldn't burn out early and making sure to drink water as well as splash it over my body during the race. He kept smiling and reassuring me that I would do fine, that the ankles would hold out, that I would finish well. And my concern was that I not let my eyes reveal too much affection for him, that I not embarrass him by exposing myself in this cordial group of Betty's friends. Not *one* of those friends would have dropped dead if it somehow became clear what I felt for this man. As an old high school friend said recently when I confessed to being gay, "I'm never offended by people being what they are." But I didn't let my face reveal my feelings. For the thousandth time, as I shook his hand goodbye, I resolved to say how I felt about someone even if the love is sure to go unrequited. I didn't stand much chance of enjoying the party if I went through life afraid to even *ask* someone for a dance.

In the nearly twenty years of our friendship William has slept with someone else only once, an old lover who happened to come through town. At least this is what he tells me, and I believe him. Monogamy was a gift he chose to give me, to prove the depth of his love for me. (Never any dearth of men and women both who would have jumped at the chance with him. Once we came home and found a lady had broken into the house. When we couldn't talk her into leaving, and it became evident she was not well, we had to call the local policeman to help us get her back home to the asylum. There was always some student mooning about wanting to have the great man's baby or just looking for a Princeton rub and a good grade. Star fucking, I believe Wystan Auden or Chester used to call it.)

But those years when our work kept William and me apart much of the time he never expected me to be celibate. He only never wanted to know the details. It hurt him when he knew, and the pain divided us. Because he offered me this freedom I never felt trapped in the friendship and was probably a lot less promiscuous in the old days than I might normally have been. When we came together there were no strings attached, a sort of perpetual courtship where we were on our best behavior all the time. Were we less "committed" to each other than people in a "real" marriage? I don't think so. Gays and straights are always trying to force the concept of heterosexual marriage onto the sort of life two men lead together, and it's a mistake. Round peg, square hole.

The most you can say is that William and I have stuck by each other over the long haul, and I'm proud of that. A poem William wrote for me a long time ago comes close to the mystery of it:

TREE MARRIAGE

In Chota Nagpur and Bengal
the betrothed are tied with threads to
mango trees, they marry the trees
as well as one another, and
the two trees marry each other.
Could we do that some time with oaks
or beeches? This gossamer we
hold each other with, this web
of love and habit is not enough.
In mistrust of heavier ties,
I would like tree-siblings for us,
standing together somewhere, two
trees married with us, lightly, their
fingers barely touching in sleep,
our threads invisible but holding.

I don't think I've ever met a more generous person in my life. All summer long the dear old guy puttered around filling the hours alone while I did my runs and kept my journal. All weekend he agreed to be hauled around the streets of New York, pushed into the hurly-burly of marathon weekend. I promised myself again that when the race was run I would work on his exercises and speech therapy every day, come hell or high water.

Once we were back at Betty's I checked her answering machine and made a final call to see if I could track down Peter Weller. I'd have to leave him a note and hope he had a key for her house if he wanted to stay there. Fate was conspiring to make this a very personal running affair.

I gave up trying to decide what I would wear for the race and left three different outfits out to choose from in the morning. If it was really cold, I'd take a jacket and get rid of it as the day heated up. If it was only brisk, I'd wear the cotton T-shirt they gave out. And if it was warm, I'd only wear a nylon tank top. I decided to forget the micro tape recorder, the Band-Aids, the Vaseline, and all the other paraphernalia I'd stuffed into my red pouch. My only concession to technology would be the radio headphones I'd come to depend on to pull me up the hills with the rhythms of hard rock. I would be running naked, free, through all five boroughs, just out for a spin through streets lined with thousands of New Yorkers. It would be a day to enjoy. I went in and cuddled up to William. He said the "Our Father" to me, and I fell into a deep sleep.

PART THREE

THE RUN

November 1 — New York City
Marathon Day

"Well, this is it," I said out loud when I woke at 7:30. "D day." I sat on the edge of the bed aware that I had been dreaming just minutes before, but I couldn't remember the dream. Whatever the dreadful details, I had cleaned myself of all my anxiety and felt fresh as the crisp autumn morning that was pouring light through the bedroom window. The red cardinal on Betty's outside thermometer was perched at fifty degrees. It was going to be perfect weather for a marathon. William lay in a rumpled ball, warm, snoring softly like a purring cat. I hated to wake him, but since his stroke his morning routine takes nearly two hours by the time he showers, shaves, and eats breakfast, and Grace had said she would come for us at nine.

"Hey, bud, it's time to get up," I said, shaking his shoulders gently.

Sometimes he's way in deep and even after his eyes are open he doesn't seem to focus on the world for a few minutes. But the first thing he invariably says when I wake him is "All right, sir," with a willingness and attention that must have come from all those years of duty as a pilot. I'm such an ogre in the morning that his good will always breaks my heart a little, especially when I consider the challenge he faces each day just to interpret the world and do what it required of him.

I headed for the bathroom, limping a little, the ankle pain now chronic in the morning. The microtears in the tendons and fascia connecting the bones just hadn't had enough time to heal. "If I can warm up and forget the pain, and if the tendon doesn't snap," I thought to myself as I sat on the stool. But the ankle wasn't really a worry now in some ways. For months I had trained and done the best I could. Now I would watch it all unfold as though I were watching a movie. I had achieved every goal in the training up till now, and if my injury didn't knock me out, I was *scheduled* to have enough stamina to finish. The anticipation building in my gut was like the jitters you feel the first day of the new school year. There isn't anything you can do about it, so you might as well put on your new shoes and go out and see who is on the school bus.

The relief I felt when I got up to start the shower was more than physical. Runners get a little anal obsessive, and a perfectly formed ten-incher can start your day better than a good horoscope or winning the lottery. Aside from the comfort you feel running after a healthy BM, you also don't have to worry about babying a nervous diarrhea while you are trying to get through a grueling 26.2-mile race. Who can forget the stupid novice sportscaster who kept announcing of the female front-runner, "It looks like she's bleeding, the backs of her legs are all streaked, it looks like she's bleeding," until a more senior announcer said, "No, she's okay," and focused his commentary on another runner. A woman who's run twenty miles in a couple of hours is like a beautiful racehorse driving home with animal instinct. The niceties aren't going to keep her from her goal of winning. But losing control of your bowels in front of millions of spectators is not something anyone looks forward to if it can be avoided.

Normally, I save a hot shower for after the morning run. I like to let my body come awake in the process of working up a sweat and getting the blood up to the brain. Besides, there's something kind of nice about the smell of our own bodies in the morning before they get sanitized and deodorized and we go out into our civilized day.

This year I bought Mikey an L.L. Bean bed, a rust-colored pillow filled with cedar chips about as big as the Red Sea. Sometimes I catch him lying on his back, all four legs in the air, pretending to be asleep, and I sneak into his bed on my knees. Nothing nicer than the smell of a warm dog asleep in a ball. And he returns the compliment. The smell of my sweat socks drives him so crazy I have to go out on the deck if I want to get my sneakers on in the morning without his knocking me over. A little kinky, maybe, but as my father says, "You'll *have* this."

Since I'd be running with Grace, I decided to get myself all cleaned up and be a little social. In a half hour I stood naked in front of Betty's full-length mirror inspecting the results. This was the first year my tan line took the shape of a pair of running shorts, and my butt was baby white, like a giant bean pod blossoming on two brown stalks. My hair was getting a little thin at the temples, and the mustache came off earlier in the summer, but it was still a pretty strong face: green eyes, substantial nose, thick brown lashes and eyebrows.

What do you make of your own face? How can you read it? What does it seem like to others? How does character enter into some, while others seem unformed even at death? A stockbroker friend used to spend three minutes in front of the mirror each morning repeating to himself, "You can *do* it," and would start his day off looking like a samurai warrior in a three-piece suit. No' thank you.

"Not getting any flashier," William says of his own body in a poem. Not getting any flashier, maybe me either. It always kind of surprises me when a checkout girl starts flirting or someone looks me up and down on the beach. Not a young body anymore. I could not pass for twenty-one if a Studio 54 bouncer checked ID's to keep out people over thirty. Still, the shoulders were broad, the thighs bulging, and incredibly there was now no easily perceivable gut, or at least I barely had to suck the gut in at all for it to disappear.

Sister Marguerite used to tell the story of a waitress getting fed up with a truck driver who kept asking for more sugar for his coffee. "Honey," said the exasperated waitress, "stir up what you *got.*" Well, all summer I'd stirred it up with single-minded determination, and I had to admit it was not the body of the man who had started this project two months ago. Old Betty had done it again. There I stood, Mr. Clean inside and out, tan, shaved, purged, fresh as a sacrificial virgin standing at the edge of a volcano crater.

I heard William banging cabinet doors out in the kitchen, and I decided I'd better go out and rummage for a little breakfast too. All the pasta I'd been eating for the past few days was going to have to do me, like a bear living off his fat during the winter.

This morning I would only have a little OJ, maybe some tea and toast to give nervous stomach juices something to work on. I debated taking a couple of Advil to reduce the inflammation in my heel the way I'd done in San Diego. If I finished this marathon, though, I wanted it to be my own victory, not like the triumph of some machine in the NFL running on steroids, painkiller, and maybe even some cocaine to give him a little psychological edge. I figured if I stayed within the prescribed dosage on the back of the bottle, two tablets every four hours, I'd still be able to keep the medal they hang on your neck if you cross the finish line. I put two additional tablets in a plastic sandwich bag along with twenty dollars in small bills, a couple of Band-Aids, and a slip of paper giving my name and telephone number at Paul's house in case there was a problem. It was only a remote possibility, of course. It was rare for a runner to drop dead of a heart attack while running, though it did occasionally occur. The worst that could probably happen to me would be heat exhaustion, or maybe something broken here or there, but a good scout is always prepared.

Your task was to beat gravity, beat the erosion of the body's resources by willpower, take yourself beyond the Wall. You couldn't carry all the paraphernalia needed for the job; you had to depend on others for fluid replacement or health care, or even to monitor you from without to see if you were getting yourself into trouble inside without even knowing it. And if you were getting into trouble, you had to depend on luck and the help of strangers like a patient entering the operating room and hoping for the best. Perhaps that was the nature of the strange, symbiotic relationship between the crowds on the sidelines and the crowds running, a kind of mutual need. The adult play our rabbi was talking about last night. The stupid runner had agreed to try to exceed what might normally be a safe athletic distance to run, to risk his health a little and go beyond the normal—sharpening his spirit like a matador teasing a bull, kicking death in the shins a little. The crowd had agreed to watch and lend a hand if necessary.

But running a marathon wasn't just for heroically endowed

athletes. Twenty-two thousand very normal people would be out there giving it everything they had and more. The news media misses the whole point every year by only concentrating on fancy pros who win the race. The people support this race, the *crowds* stay out in the street, because for every grandmother or teenage kid who makes it in after four or eight hours, there are ten spectators on the sidelines who would run the race if they could and realize they might just be *able* to if the chunky character coming up the hill a few feet away has decided to try it. When someone in the crowd calls out, "You can do it," he is really saying, "*We* can do it," or even "I can do it."

And maybe the runner, like Walter Mitty, is saying to himself, "Lay it on, you Nazi bastard, I'll never tell you the names of the Resistance leaders," as he daydreams through the final miles of the race. Serious play. He could probably make it with his own imagination, but the roar of a million real-life New Yorkers, as a runner crosses the bridge from Queens into Manhattan, is about as big a kick in the pants any athlete is ever going to get in life no matter what the sport or forum. Well. I tucked my ID slip, my emergency supplies, and my Walter Mitty daydreams into a sandwich baggie and folded the packet into the change pocket in my shorts. Grace and her husband Rudy had just pulled into the driveway, and it was time to get the show on the road.

I greeted them at the little stoop to the front door and felt as though I were welcoming friends that we'd known for years. When William and I meet new people some of them read him instinctively, and treat him with affection right off the bat. He's winning and easy to like, but not everyone perceives his value or takes the extra effort it requires to include him in a conversation. It's more than just good manners. I've discovered that the way new acquaintances meet William is something of a litmus test for their own character. A joy when we come across such new friends.

Grace was a vision of pink, right down to her fingernails. I was about to say toenails and tell a little artistic lie about seeing her pinkies as she adjusted her sports orthotics. There are plenty of little embellishments that could be added to this account to prop up the prose a little. But for better or worse, I want this to be as faithful a description of the training and running of the New York City Marathon on November 1 as my notes and memory can provide. I always like it when the credits come up after a movie and I discover that this has been a "true story," that the bad guys have all gone to jail, and the heroine is living happily ever after somewhere in the south of France. Besides, my running the marathon is certainly one case where truth is stranger than fiction.

Anyhow, the four of us took turns taking photographs of one another, and Grace had a couple of nervous pees as we got ready to go.

"Richard, I don't think you're going to need that jacket," she said. "It's going to heat up beautiful today."

"You really don't think so?"

"Nah, you'll just wind up throwing it away."

I had bought the designer running suit in one of those counterfeit clothes markets you find in the Philippines, and there were too many memories connected with the coat to ever throw it away. For months I had worked in a remote clinic servicing personnel at the nuclear power plant being built by Westinghouse in the shade of a volcano close to a fault line in the Bataan Peninsula. It was an armed camp, really, and I was one of the few inmates stupid enough to venture outside the walls. One night when I was jogging I even met a cobralike character in camouflage fatigues who I'm sure was one of the guerrillas vowing that the plant would never go on-line. He seemed as bored as I was and just kept smoking his cigarette as he disappeared into a field of bamboo.

It was a difficult assignment. I made mistakes, and nearly got eaten up by enemies on the inside of the camp. But I survived. My running suit was a reminder of days more exotic and more naive, the uniform of a certain type of adult determination. I might need it today in more ways than one. I stuffed the jacket into my hand luggage and slammed the door of Betty's house as we walked to the car.

Grace and I jumped out at the police barrier and made our

farewells to Rudy and William. Kisses, handshakes, hugs. You'd have thought we were about to set off on an around-the-world cruise. Grace instructed us to meet after the race under the letter X in the family reunion area, since there wouldn't be many people with a last name beginning with X.

"Grace, what's to guarantee five thousand other runners won't have the same idea?" her husband asked.

"They will, only they'll decide five thousand other runners will have the same idea so they'll go to the letter they're supposed to meet at."

"Oh," he said. X would mark the spot. But to avoid pneumonia, we agreed that we wouldn't wait more than a half hour for each other after the finish.

"Wish me good luck," I said to William.

"Luck," he said, and waved his right hand, a small crumpled fist he makes when he gets excited or is concentrating on something difficult.

Fort Wadsworth Park was a mob scene, as though a Super Bowl football stadium had emptied out onto its staging fields. Runners were converging from all parts of the world and from all points of the compass. The morning chill was already beginning to burn off, and runners were stripping themselves of plastic bags and old sweats. A number of runners sported less-than-traditional outfits. Two were dressed head to foot in Arab robes and veils and paraded around like Saudi royalty. One black boy was dressed like a French chef with a cream puff hat, apron, and white uniform. He even carried a three-layered wedding cake, which I hoped for his sake was made of cardboard. Six guys formed the twelve legs of a fairly realistic centipede snaking around a flatbed trailer on which drill sergeants directed warm-up exercises. It was hard to tell if the more exotic running outfits were a result of the Halloween holiday, or if some esoteric statement was being made. Carnival.

The prerace material had announced, "There will be more than three hundred portable toilets and the world's longest urinal at the start. Please don't use the bushes!" There were such long lines, however, that every tree larger than a fire hydrant was occupied. Grace kept marching from one john to another, sure we would find one that had shorter lines. But when we came to the main tent she decided we should check in first and tap a kidney later. We fed ourselves into roped-off funnels leading into the tent. At the end of each line a volunteer stood with an electronic wand that she ran over the code strip at the bottom of our bib number. The wand made a little beep when it got the number, like a fancy checkout register at the grocery store that "reads" your purchases and gives you a computer printout of the price of peas.

As we rang through the line the volunteer bean counters wished us good luck, then Grace and I queued up for the johns beyond the tent. The doors on the little houses were marked "Men" or "Women," but the distinction had long since become academic as both sexes shifted from one leg to another in anticipation. No sooner did a runner come out, bursting into breath like a whale surfacing from the ocean depths, than another runner hustled into the foul box, regardless of the designated gender on the door. This was not a polite line of beauties clutching their evening bags during intermission at *Aida*. It was like elbowing your way through a shopping center the day after Christmas as groups funneled their way into single file. Runners just coming on the line were nervous. You could feel the latecomers willing the lucky occupant to get on with it. As they got closer to their goal, however, runners in the front of the line became sweetness and light, since now it was clear they'd make it before the call to the start. Occasionally, a round of applause sounded for some sluggard whose olfactory nerve was apparently shot but who finally released his booth for someone else.

"How's your ankle feeling today?" Grace asked from the line she was standing in.

"It's a little less stiff, but it still hurts. There's no way I'll do this nonstop, I guess."

"I pulled my knee last week," the girl in front of me began.

"Your ankle will warm up," Grace said. "Just keep moving, Richard, no matter what. Don't let your body go into a walk, keep jogging even if you're going slow as a snail. Once you stop running it's hard to get started up again."

"Twenty-six miles is a long way, Grace."

"Forget twenty-six miles," she said. "Just think of one mile at a time until you float across the finish line. Peachy." She gave me a little punch in the stomach.

From time to time a pleasant young guy came on the PA system to tell us how much time we had left, making announcements about the day. "Here comes the Goodyear blimp, ladies and gentlemen, that cigar-shaped cloud just coming over the Verrazano Bridge. What a view they must have up there."

People spread over the fields of Fort Wadsworth like a Hollywood movie set of Moses leading his people out of Egypt. I'd never seen such a crowd before, a World Series sell-out where everyone in the stadium is a player. The expectation in the runners was almost visible.

"Ladies and gentlemen, please don't forget to keep drinking lots of water. It's going to be plenty warm today, so you've got to keep replacing those fluids."

Tables were set up everywhere, honeycombed with paper cups that water boys and girls replenished from thirty-gallon cans.

"Now, ladies and gentlemen, we're going to get going here in just a few minutes. We want all the men with runner numbers under 15,999 to begin at the blue start. All other runners will begin at the red start. Please don't go onto the bridge plaza until your start color has been called. We're going to give you plenty of time to get to the starting line, so when we call you please move gently. When you are called, line up near the pace sign that indicates your predicted finish time for the marathon."

If I could average 10 minutes for each mile, I figured I could finish in 260 minutes—60 into 260, 6 into 26—let's see, my estimated time would be 4 hours and 20 minutes. With an extra 10 minutes for the 0.2 miles added by the queen cheering from her balcony, and it looked as though I might run the marathon in 4 ½ hours, just what I had signed up for. Clever, the way they print out your schedule for you upside down at the bottom of your bib number so you can read it as you run: 5 miles at 51 minutes; 10 miles at 1 hour and 43 minutes; half marathon at 2 hours 15 minutes; 20 miles at 3 hours 26 minutes; 25 miles at 4 hours 17 minutes; and finish in 4 hours and 30 minutes. I wouldn't be burning up the track at that pace, but it was as fast as I'd gone on my longest run. I wondered if 10-minute miles would be realistic for 26 miles.

"Okay, folks," the announcer called out. "This is what we've all been waiting for. Would the red starters please begin to move onto the toll plaza. And slowly, please. We won't be going anywhere until everyone is in place."

A tidal wave of 4,489 women and several thousand men swelled over the little knoll to the toll plaza and lined up behind the pace signs strung on poles high over the crowd. I looked for the sign that indicated ten-minute miles. Happily, there were men and women, young and old, who also planned on a four-and-a-half-hour marathon. There were plenty of runners with such modest expectations among the blue starters as well, but as this was my first marathon I was placed with the women. For the first eight miles the red and blue runners would run a parallel but separate course. At Lafayette Avenue, however, red and blue starters would join up together for the rest of the marathon.

When the blue runners were called to the start with the red, it was like standing in the middle of a beehive, a general buzz of nervous chatter and good wishes almost overwhelming the PA system. At the instructions of the announcer, runners began passing clothes they wished to discard to the sidelines. Old sweats went hand over hand like beers at a ball game. Twins from Arizona decided their long-sleeved tops would be too hot, and we all joined around to rip their arms off. Very little sweat-shirt was left to cover the leopard brassieres they wore underneath.

"Don't you think gloves are going to be a little warm?" I asked a nice-looking black kid in front of me. He wore skintight shorts and a little beanie. I wondered if maybe he had turned up at the wrong event.

"Yeah, I guess you're right," he said. He took off his gloves and tucked them into his shorts at the waist.

I worried about the fancy pants. After a few miles they could cut off his circulation better than a tourniquet. But then I noticed discreet zippers sewn into the seams along the thighs.

The nasal foghorn of Mayor Ed Koch cut through the hubbub to get the attention of the runners. This was a politician's dream, and the mayor milked it for all it was worth. The welcome was real New York—big, warm, exaggerated, and gaudy, like a bear hug from Elizabeth Taylor.

When I first moved to Brooklyn years ago to begin medical studies, the first thing I saw on the street was a boy in a ducktail addressing a friend who was having difficulty getting into a parking space. "Whahs a matter? Ya stupid or something?" he asked. Over the years I came to realize that that was Brooklynese for "Hi, Jimmy. How are you doing today?"

Helicopters were hovering in place over the Verrazano Bridge, and several blimps floated up a little higher. Sailboats glided up and down the river, tugs passed under the bridge spraying jets of water hundreds of feet into the air. At the very top of the bridge perhaps fifty lilliputian-sized cameramen were filming the human ribbon that lay at their feet waiting to unwind. A string of sailors holding hands stretched across the starting line like a paper cutout. As the good mayor fired up his hyperbole my nerves got the better of me. I stopped listening and felt my eyes start to sting. The whole scene was as overwhelming as they promised. I had lost my personality, felt small and inconsequential, but in a mystical way somehow I was powerful—powerful as the whole of the human mass that had come together for this event, like the core of a nuclear reactor going critical. One body, one voice. A lot of people around me felt the same way. It wouldn't have mattered, but I didn't want the beauty of what I was feeling to start me crying. It was like trying to stop the hiccups by an act of will until a good scare does the trick.

Boom. (William says exclamation marks are archaic on the page, that language must be strong enough to convey the emotion.) Well, boom! The cannon scared me shitless, as they say, and I no longer had to worry about my dignity.

For five minutes we ran in place like a hoard of Chinese foot soldiers until the thousands ahead of us began to move across the bridge. Finally the wind whispered to us, the dragon's tail came alive, and we were off.

"Have a good journey," Grace said to me, careful of the word "journey" as though she had been waiting to give me a secret piece of advice. "Been nice knowing you," we used to say in the old days as we lifted a glass of bourbon. There wouldn't be anything artificial about our recreation today, though—this was to be the ultimately natural, maybe once-in-a-lifetime high. She gave me the sly big Bancroft smile, and I pulled her up for a kiss. I also made the sign of the cross the way we used to do before leaving the locker room at halftime, the way I still do when I'm sure the plane is going to crash. My heart was speeding at a rate that had nothing to do with running. The sun was bright, the air sharp, and the water all diamonds below us. We couldn't ask for a better day.

"*Look* at those guys," Grace said in feigned disgust at the two hundred men who had stopped along the railing and turned their backs to the runners going by. "You know they just saved it up so they could say they had a pee off the Verrazano Bridge."

"Penis envy, Grace," I said.

"Ha. I've seen women stop too."

Occasionally, someone would accidentally tramp on the person in front of him or bump into a runner trying to get by. It was a little disconcerting to be in such a crowd of people having to depend on the common sense and good will of the pack to move things along safely. The queasiness of driving on an L.A. freeway. This crowd was a sample of humanity like any other, though, and sometimes the accident was no accident at all. Some creep would push by, passing on the right, say, as he bumped his way ahead: "Excuse me, I believe this is *my* stag ahead there. Or would you prefer that I rip your ear off?"

Today of all days, of course, the plastic stays in my ankle braces began to slide up and threaten to pop out as I ran. I bounced on one leg for a minute every now and then to push them back down, risking a ten-car pileup every time I did. It was impossible to move off to the side the way you were supposed to do. My ankles, especially the left, and the connective tissue to the heels were still burning like crazy, hadn't warmed up yet. It was like taking a paring knife up the side of a papaya and scraping the hard seed just under the soft flesh. The braces had pulled me through all summer, and I felt like a child whose favorite blanket had just been snatched away for the cleaners.

"These braces are giving me fits, Grace," I said, hopping on my right leg to adjust the left brace. "Listen, if I have to stop don't let me hold you back. If you want to pull out, just go ahead, okay?"

"Maybe after the bridge I'll pick up my pace," she said. Beads of sweat had formed on her upper lip.

As we came to the end of the bridge I heard a little click-click-click, and when I turned around one of the plastic struts lay on the road getting trampled by runners twenty feet behind me. Pain in the ass. But they had cost forty dollars and had saved my career as a runner this summer. I wanted to keep them.

I made my way back as though I were swimming up Niagara, a few curses hurled at me along the way. When I picked up the struts I decided to leave the damn things out, at least until I got over the bridge. I tucked the supports into the waistband at my hip. My feet felt naked, but at least I was no longer worried about being run over by ten thousand marathoners. When I looked ahead sweet Grace was just moving down the curve off the bridge. She waved and gave me the last big smile I would see till the race was over. I was on my own.

Some purists consider running with radio earphones to be antisocial, like going to a town meeting and reading a newspaper. All summer long, though, good rock and roll had helped me stave off pain and boredom as I ran the deserted country roads in Connecticut. Sometimes a particularly pounding Rolling Stones song carried me into another lap just as I was about to give it up for the day. Music had become as indispensable as my ankle braces. When Grace disappeared down the exit ramp onto 92nd Street I tuned in my headset as though I were lighting up a good Cuban cigar after a pound and a half of rare prime rib.

Ah, those were the days, weren't they? We never thought of cholesterol, or lung cancer, or angioplasty. It never crossed our minds that vegetarians were less likely to suffer from gallstones, that calorie needs decreased with age, that before you added salt

to your meal at the table you should probably at least *taste* your
food to see if it was needed. The worst that could happen from a
night of debauchery in the Big Apple could be cured with a shot
or two of penicillin. It never occurred to us that Mick Jagger
would turn forty, that Diana Ross might look old one day, that
John Lennon would ever die.

　　But find the right song, turn it up loud enough, and there you
are again cruising down a country road to a polo game in autumn, top down on your mom's '65 Mustang, full bottle of Jack
Daniels at your side. Or you're blasting through the suburbs of
Paris on the back of a friend's motorcycle headed for the Cannes
Film Festival. He's teaching you how to ride, your arms sur-
round his black leather jacket at the waist. Better-looking than a
young Brando, and he has invited *you* for a weekend in Cannes.
How will you hide the crush that is growing as you fly into the
wind down to the Côte d'Azur holding on tight to your friend?
Strawberry fields forever.

　　Running with a radio didn't take you out of the race, it just
added to the joy of the ride. It was like a good movie score that
helped your heart follow the action. Aretha Franklin was de-
manding a little R-E-S-P-E-C-T when I danced off the bridge
and landed in Bay Ridge. By then I had become mesmerized by
a girl dressed in metallic green running shorts. On each cheek of
her well-endowed derriere she had printed the word "go" in
large gold letters, and watching her run was like having a private
cheering section: go go, go go, go go.

　　I wasn't ready for the throng that greeted us when we came
off the bridge—a rambunctious crowd lining the sidewalks. This
is a working neighborhood of Irish and Italian and mostly
Norwegians, who first came here in 1636 fleeing religious perse-
cution. "Ten thousand Swedes lay in the weeds all chased by one
Norwegian" is a rhyme you might hear as children jumped rope.
Each May 17 the neighborhood still celebrates Norwegian Independence Day. Anything for a party.

　　Half the guys in the crowd pulled on a can of beer, women
too. Little old ladies sat waving from cheap folding chairs in
front of their row houses. The local fire station apparently had
one of their own in the race. A sentry was stationed in the bin of

a cherry picker, which telescoped from the back of a fire truck. When he picked out their boy in the crowd sirens went off, lights flashed, and the whole company went into an uproar. Mongrels of every possible genetic combination sported red and blue kerchiefs about their necks like cowboys. Some had balloons tied to their collars. Church was over, the day was sunny, and this was the best show in town.

All along 4th Street groups of children like flocks of chicks huddled together and stuck their tiny arms into the flow of runners. Their mothers stood behind watching over what had become a ritual, like organizing a line of seven-year-olds for their first communion. This was more than just "getting five." The runners were heroes for these kids, and they wanted to touch us, simply to touch us, as though we might bring good luck or some of our strength might flow into them. I thought of that cereal advertisement that portrays gorgeous athletes working out before their morning Wheaties until the jazzy lady comes on and sings, "Go tell your mama what the *big* boys eat."

It might sound a little wacky or sentimental, but this energy surge seemed to flow both ways. We felt that we were in touch with some sort of grace or power too as we touched the children. A jogger would pull over to the side and put out his hand as he ran by, pat, pat, pat, pat, pat, pat, pat, pat, slapping all their little mitts and taking in the bright smiles, the astonishment, and sometimes the fear on the faces. He found it hard not to straighten up a little and tighten his form as he ran through this mill of glad hands.

Ahead, an army of volunteers in yellow slickers manned the first station holding water out to runners. Sweepers couldn't keep up with their numbers, and the street was paved with crushed dixie cups, making it somewhat hazardous to swing in for refreshment. We'd been encouraged to drink at every station and throw water on ourselves as well to stay cool, but I had hardly worked up a sweat four miles into the race. The volunteers seemed to be competing for customers, and no sooner did they give up their cups than they came back with others, faces full of expectation.

"Thanks," I said to the small black girl from whom I took my first drink, running in place as I downed the water. "I needed that." Her eyes widened and she looked down at her feet. You'd have thought I'd said she was more beautiful than Whitney Houston.

Running by a crowd of spectators is a like being in a zoo, only it's hard to tell which side of the bars you're on. "We watch the loping things from the zoo of ourselves," William says in a poem about ballet dancers.

I was having a great time watching the spectators watch us. Certain runners were an obvious hit: a midget running on bandy legs, three little steps for each one of mine, a guy with his hair dyed green, a well-toned sixty-year-old with canvas, brush, and an ammo belt filled with oils, painting a fairly respectable portrait of New York as he ran along. Five miles into the race, and none of the runners was in any particular distress. The burning in my ankle had subsided. Everyone was chugging along well, and the crowd sensed our ease and high hopes. No particular drama evident. But when the Jolly Green Giant, or Michelangelo, or a runner in a tuxedo and top hat came by, the crowd pointed and laughed, sending a ripple of applause up the line, as if a pack of circus dogs in clown outfits had entered the center ring.

My radio headset produced a psychological distance between me and the crowd, something like wearing dark glasses. It didn't matter, since most of the crowd's attention went to a little old lady running the race or some guy with mountainous shoulders pushing himself along in a wheelchair. There were thousands of regular, middle-aged runners like me, and I was a little shy, just as glad to be lost in the crowd. If I needed a lift, however, all I had to do was to look someone directly in the eyes, and immediately that person began to whistle, or clap, or call out to me, just me.

It was one-sided in an odd, silent way. None of us seemed to talk to the crowd, an unwritten convention whereby we must pretend to concentrate on the effort of running. But if we looked at a pretty girl or some black dude or a grandma from San Juan, somehow our eyes let them know we were proud, that we wouldn't mind hearing what they thought. The black dude would give the thumbs up, or maybe the pretty girl would still be clapping if we turned around to catch her eye again. Even at great distances, I've read, the eyes are the most distinguishing feature about a person, even more recognizable than body shape or posture. Windows of the soul indeed.

A lot of runners had their names on their shirts, and this got a rise from the audience. "All right, Mike" or "Go, Karen, looking good" would follow you along the course if you happened to be running beside Mike or Karen. And, of course, many couldn't resist making a statement on their T-shirt, from the blatantly commercial "Don White's Ford, Why Pay More?" to the blatantly personal phone number listed under "Single, great in bed." There were team shirts, his and her shirts, and shirts that portrayed the front of a penguin, the Union Jack, or Martin Luther King, Jr., standing on a mountain. A hundred or more devotees of a fashionable guru were running with the yogi's words stenciled on plain white T-shirts. The runners didn't seem overly eager to proselytize, relying on the billboards they were wearing to spread his message. These were not your standard Moonie or Hare Krishna disciples pressuring you to come feast at the temple. But I had to admit I liked the shape of the guru's mind spelled out on their T-shirts and gave him a silent blessing back.

"Om." The sound reverberates through the universe, they say, triggers an independent harmony to help check chaos, rippling through the world like circles on a pond when a stone is dropped in the center. The harmony was resonating in my soul, all right, as I ran through the crowd lined up in Walt Whitman's old neighborhood. I knew that it would be touch and go later on. But for the moment a feeling of great well-being and peace had come over me, and I was singing the body electric.

The endorphin high people talk about has never been my experience. For me, the pleasure I feel when I'm warmed up and alert and running painlessly on a bright day is more like the animal joy I see in Mikey when he's chasing sticks in the river. He would swim out into the current and paddle logs back to the

shore until he drowned if we weren't careful. He's as committed
as the bloodhound in William's poem that would carry you
across the river on his back until the cold seeped into his heart.
Whatever is going through my mind as I run may be intense, but
the very weird thing is that for hours on end I am not aware that
I am thinking it, have pretty much lost conscious personality as
though thought had a life of its own or was being spun out in the
mind of God. It's the reverse of astroprojection. Thought has
become organic, like blood perfusing my muscles as I run. I
become so much a part of the world the loneliness of being
locked inside the body never occurs to me. It's easy to become a
little anthropomorphic at such times. It isn't just the crowd
urging me on, nature itself is conspiring in my happiness. The
breeze turns cool and friendly, the day embraces me, and the
maples in Sunset Park send up banners of color, wave over the
heads of the runners.

The crowd senses something of this too, I think. The festival
is contagious. One is likely to have a good time on such a day,
maybe meet someone, get lucky. A day to follow one's instincts.

In an early book Lewis Thomas speculates, "Maybe altruism
is our most primitive attribute." William has a poem on the
subject where he describes human kindness as "the tribe's own
drink": "we've caught it over and over / the way the thirsty
ocean catches the rain." I suppose under normal circumstances
life in New York might be described as survival of the fittest, a
human desert. But on marathon day it was raining nothing but
kindness on the zoolike streets of South Brooklyn.

One of the nice diversions for me as I slipped into cruise
control and made my way down Fourth Avenue was picking and
choosing from the people in the crowd who had brought gifts for
the runners. Water was offered at the aid stations, but every so
often a spectator stood a little into the street proffering a basket
of Hershey Kisses, orange or apple slices, hard candies, grapes,
chewing gum, or sour balls. I passed up a well-heeled couple
handing out cups of fruit compote in front of their brownstone
for a couple of Red-Hot-Dollars a little kid slipped me. Some

spectators tempted us with huge jars of Vaseline, which runners dipped into and spread erotically on their crotch or nipples or wherever they had begun to chafe.

A lot of people in the crowd had set up suitcase-sized ghetto blasters to keep the runners jumping to the Pointer Sisters or Prince. Every so often, though, a full-fledged street party was under way with a live reggae band or cottage-industry rock group. The neat demarcation between spectators and runners collapsed, and you might find yourself dancing with folks who had spilled into the street. Mardi Gras in Rio. Pushcart vendors sold hamburgers, gyros, Italian sausages, shish kebabs, and any kind of beer you wanted. The smells drove me crazy. It was about lunchtime, and I could barely resist pulling out my taxi money and stopping for a quick dog and sauerkraut. But I had a more important stop to make.

In the past half hour as I ran, the nagging small sensation that announces a full bladder had become a rather big nagging sensation. I tried to remember how often they said portable johns would be set up. Sometimes an astute spectator carried a sign reading, "Pit stop, one mile" or "Johns just ahead," but I hadn't seen such a sign for some time. I could have held on a little longer, but a walled-in parking area in front of a school came along fortuitously, and I ducked behind the wall.

It's pretty hard to pee while jogging in place, so I decided to put aside my purist notions and stood fast there behind the wall in blessed relief. It felt odd to stop the rhythm of running. It was also a little disconcerting that my urine had turned pink. A year ago when I first found out I had cancer of the bladder, that had been the first symptom. The urologist discounted the symptom as overly athletic sexual activity: "Happens all the time in young men, nothing to worry about." But when the urine turned the color of Gallo Hearty Burgundy another urologist decided to investigate the question a little more carefully.

The doctor was very happy to inform me that mine was one of the least malevolent forms of cancer, but I found that little consolation. True, I wasn't dying of AIDS, but the nasty tumor in the bladder often returned. I might lose a kidney someday, or have to be refitted with plastic plumbing. It might even be the thing that ultimately does me in. On the other hand, it might never return at all.

Our old friend Jules Hallum has written poems about the act of dying in World War as good as anything I've read. "We all get our turn," he's fond of saying about the inevitable meeting with the Grim Reaper. But you age a little when you know you're closer in line to your appointment. You begin to take stock and plan a little more carefully for the future. It scared and saddened me when my own dear parents insisted on being there for my operation. It seemed wrong that they should feel responsibility for me even into their own old age. But they said they were coming whether I liked it or not. I guess you never stop being a parent no matter how old you become.

My friend May was promised by a poet friend that she would be young forever—not biologically or chronologically but the way it really matters, he said, spiritually. She gets furious when death comes sniffing around in her life and threatens to turn her into an old woman. She won't give an inch. I tell her she'll always be beautiful, wrinkles or no, that I'd rather have dinner with Melina Mercouri than Madonna any day of the week, and that I bet if the truth were known, Ms. Mercouri would prove to be the better woman in other social encounters as well, despite Madonna's lace jumpsuits and tassled brassieres.

Dueling scars are no longer fashionable, but it doesn't make us less attractive, I think, to admit that life has touched us. Often the contrary is true. You have to be able to sense when something really has you at risk. You have to try to be a little balanced and keep things in perspective. Auden told the story of Bert Savoy, the famous female impersonator, who was watching a thunderstorm with some friends. " 'There's Miss God at it again,' Bert exclaimed and was instantly struck dead by lightning."

This time around, as I inspected the Gallo Rosé splashing against the wall, I felt pretty certain I had just traumatized myself a little by running with a full bladder and made a mental note to stop more often. Go to the back of the line, your turn hasn't come up yet. But the pit stop made it clear why I'd been warned to keep moving, no matter what. In the two minutes I stood ruminating on meeting my maker all my muscles decided to freeze up as though they'd suddenly become aware of what I was putting them through. I longed to sit down for a minute. Auden's words came to me again, a late poem in which the flesh is "praying for Him to die, / so setting Her free to become / irresponsible Matter."

It isn't too hard to talk yourself into keeping at it when fatigue and pain tempt you to stop. It's very tough, however, to get back in gear once you've stopped running and the oxygen-starved muscles finally get a breather. It's like being frozen in a block of ice and having to break out by an act of will. Mind over matter, one of those times that prove the marathon is more a spiritual than physical challenge. The tendons in your groin, hip joints, and calves catch fire like silk rent by flame. Experience tells you the agony will eventually pass, but first you must walk through the fire and immolate your pain.

Offer it up, take a cold shower, try to think of something else, the nuns would counsel when the temptation of sins of the flesh came up on the agenda during my boyhood. As I ran I tried to forget my aches and pains by using the same distraction technique. I concentrated on remembering what part of the course I'd come to as I turned down Bedford Avenue. The Marathon Guide said I'd be "following the footsteps of history," that this was to be a first-class history course as well as a premier race course, so I had to pay attention and enjoy the lesson.

If I remembered rightly, I had already passed the Fort Greene monument for the Prison Ship Martyrs. Eleven thousand colonists had died on British ships docked in Wallabout Bay during the Revolutionary War, about half as many as were running in the race today, a toll hard to imagine from that faraway, romantic war. How many of these poor ghosts trailed the runners like unseen coaches in the core of their fatigue?

If the guide was right, I ought to be coming into Williamsburg, where "Brooklyn's booming industrial section got its start." When they opened the bridge in 1903, however, the diaspora made it perhaps the largest settlement of Hasidic Jews in the world, and sure enough little family groups of Hasidim stood like flocks of starlings along the sidelines viewing the race in silence. The men wore black fedoras to cover their yarmulkes, black coats and trousers with white shirts buttoned to the neck. Many wore beards, and single foot-long locks of hair fell in front of their ears like ropes to pull them to Abraham's bosom. The women were dressed in equally drab attire. Dark stockings, skirts, and sweaters covered every bit of skin save the face, which was naked of makeup or even natural expression. Only the children revealed their parents' love of life, pride in family. The exquisite creatures were dressed in crushed velvet, subtle navy-blue or forest-green capes trimmed in black with fine stockings and shoes. The curl locks on the men looked goofy, but on the boys were quite precious. Their faces were bowls of cream set with cherry cheeks and coal-black eyes. They were the most beautiful children I had ever seen, with an unworldly aura of privacy about them. You could almost feel the effort it took to overcome shyness and offer a runner a piece of orange or a candy. Their parents would coax them into the street for the exceptional encounter, their black eyes luminous with excitement under thick lashes. When a runner accepted their gift they jumped back to their mothers like little crickets, filled with surprise and pleasure.

Williamsburg was certainly the quietest stretch of spectators so far, but the silent intensity as they stared at us or offered dignified applause made me feel as though we'd done something important. Serious work, liebling. Congratulations.

Polish and Russian immigrants had set up shop in the community of Greenpoint next door to the Jews of Williamsburg, and it was a far livelier crowd that greeted us as we ran down McGuinness Avenue. Gold onion domes competed with Gothic steeples on the skyline. Lampposts were decorated with red, white, and blue balloons. The residents were very good at parades, had a highly developed "sense of occasion," as Chester Kallman used to say. In 1969 a little-known Polish archbishop made a triumphant visit to this community. Some years later a local street was rechristened John Paul II Square when he became pope. Just ahead the Pulaski Bridge, named for the Polish hero of the American Revolutionary War, marked the halfway point of the marathon—13.1 miles and feeling good again after my pit stop. The body was running smoothly, with the normal level of pain in the left ankle.

My right hip had developed a burning ache to compensate, I suppose, for my favoring the weak ankle. A hernialike pain began to flare up in the appendix area when I thought about it, but my form hadn't gone out of whack in any serious way. There was no discounting the fatigue, though. Mid-marathon, I sure felt I had spent more than half of myself in the race. Today was certainly going to require a marathon effort. *There's* a new adjective for you, Richard, I thought, to qualify the rare, sustained, and extraordinarily difficult. A marathon friendship, or a marathon marriage. "I couldn't bear the party," one might sigh with hyperbolic flare. "It was *marathon* boredom." Or "Have you seen the new tax forms this year? Absolutely marathon."

A middle-aged woman tugged on my shirt-sleeve trying to pull me out of my rumination. A group of young blacks on the corner started cheering and throwing fists into the air. "Who's ahead?" she shouted again, when I took off my earphones.

Just a little more than two hours into the race it was incredible to think that someone had just proved victorious when I still had better than half the race to run. I put on my headset again and was able to tune in to the sports announcement.

"Some guy from Ethiopia has already won it. Two hours and eleven minutes. Ibrahim Hussein or something like that."

"Yeah, yeah," she said. "What about the *women?* Who's leading the women?"

"I didn't catch it," I shouted to her. The lady had fifteen years on me easy, but she pulled away like a mildly bored Porsche owner leaving a Pontiac Firebird in the dust.

The dark horse among the women in today's race would later be described by *Running News* this way: "Priscilla Welch's strategy, to go out fast and literally get lost among the men, worked to perfection. She was invisible for most of the race, constantly obscured by an ever-shifting phalanx of half-a-dozen men. . . . But receive a trophy she did, arriving at the finish in 2:30:17, a long shot away from the other women." At forty-two, Priscilla Welch is one year my senior. Gulp.

I wondered if the crowds would begin to drift away now that the race had been won, but there didn't seem to be any rush to empty the streets. There were still thousands to watch us stomp over the metal grating of the Pulaski Bridge. I liked watching the runners myself. Once again I was savoring the attraction of bodies in running gear, the silky shorts cut high above a runner's thighs, the simple T-shirt or tank top, the goofy shoes that flatten out like duck feet. I passed one guy in bright green tights, red sneaks, and a white tank top, part of the Italian contingent. In a way he was more naked than if he hadn't been wearing anything.

Once when I was jogging with Betty an elderly woman stopped her car at a green light to let us cross.

"That was civil of her, wasn't it?" I puffed.

"She just wanted to get a good look at your butt," Betty explained.

"Go on. She could be my grandmother."

"The rear end's the best part. Do men stop looking when they get old?" She gives me these tips on the opposite sex from time to time, "warns me about thieves and moths and women / nothing for money, all for neighborhood," as William says of Mrs. Lemmington in that poem about his country neighbor.

In spite of all the good will from the fans lining the streets of Brooklyn and Queens, I was beginning to wonder if Manhattan was ever going to appear at the end of the rainbow. I'd been at it for two and a half hours now, about as long as I'd ever run before, and I was beginning to feel as though I were in one of those dreams where you fall and fall and fall and never have the satisfaction of hitting earth.

A lot of runners were beginning to show some wear and tear now, and the encouragement from the spectators was genuine, not the bright congratulation thrown out earlier in the race when we were still fresh and optimistic. Pain and sweat streaked the runners' faces. Some panted or made little cries as they favored an injury or simply pushed against gravity. The fans got a little louder, a little more insistent when some poor soul came struggling by doing his or her best not to let the pain win. The blind guy who was chatting up a storm with his running partner just a few miles back tagged along in silence and only reached out occasionally to touch his partner for bearings.

It was something like having the flu. You feel just awful. How does the old chestnut go? "First I was afraid I was going to die, then I was afraid I wasn't." But unlike children who have no sense of history and cry all night with an earache because they can't imagine a world without earache, adults are able to endure pain because they have experienced earaches before, can extrapolate their personal history. All they have to do is *forget* the exploding eardrum for twelve or fifteen hours, and by sunrise it will all be over.

Very simple.

Perhaps the weirdest sensation was to have an exquisite pain whose source I couldn't identify. More than the awful heaviness, it felt as though some window decorator had skewered my thighs with metal ramrods to support some particularly lurid pose. I couldn't exactly visualize where the trouble was coming from, and was like a paraplegic who has to reach down to feel if the accident has left him with any legs. Pain is a very difficult serpent to trace as it slithers through the body's high grasses. A man with severe prostatitis only knows the agony begins below the belly button, a lady with gallstones may feel certain she is dying of uterine cancer. How little we know of what goes on between our neck and our knees. The pain we suffer is like orgasm, each time unique, mysterious, without replication. Describing it is like explaining sight to a blind person. Even the skilled anatomist has difficulty connecting the reality of what the body is feeling inside with the color maps he is able to devise for the body's geography.

As I meditated on the curious state of my upper thighs, a part of me sat down in an easy chair and pulled out the old notes from my first surgical rotation. In my mind I flipped through the various diagrams I'd drawn to see if they offered any clues. Fractures, vein stripping, different sorts of tumors and the various procedures to accommodate their individual growth patterns. And then, ah-ha, I was finally able to put a picture with the pain I felt.

A "hip replacement" is only a funny term for gluing a peg with a silver ball into the upper femur and slipping the restored piece back into the hip socket—it's like carpentry, simple as plugging a new caster into a rickety office chair. It sounded a little medieval when you explained it to patients, but the operation had those octogenarians walking around good as new time after time. When they first came in they always described the same type of amorphous pain that was warming my own hips and legs as I ran on the streets of Queens. It looked as though the extra pounds I'd been carrying around these past few years were finally beginning to warp my body's architecture, and the girders were sagging a little.

I thought of my favorite deejay in D.C., an old black dude named Jerry Washington who spins the blues on Saturday mornings. Nothing better to start off your day on a weekend. I put on my headphones and Mikey and I start up the neighborhood hills, running with the Howlin' Wolf, Otis Redding, Sam Cooke, or maybe Lightning Hopkins, and the music warms my soul like a bush burning for Moses. The blues pour through me and I want to cry, "Oh, my prophetic soul."

For the millionth time I asked myself why I had gotten into this mess. I wondered if some degree of masochism was a prerequisite for trying to run a marathon, the way, at a very deep subliminal level, a thin thread of sadism must run through the psyche of the surgeon.

Fifteen miles into the race, however, if there was some unconscious, more esoteric reason why I was putting myself through all this, I'd have given anything for a clever psychologist to pop out from the sidelines and tell me what it was.

An English pundit writing about the London Marathon recently describes it as mass idiocy, the looniness of the long-distance runner. "We are not talking here about a few blisters, a stitch, and a temporary urge to expectorate heart, lungs and stomach. We are talking of hypothermia and hyperthermia; of tissue exhaustion and debilitating dehydration; of torn muscles, snapped tendons, fractured bones; of long-term damage to joints, bringing the risk of arthritis; of blood blisters requiring toenails to be punctured with red-hot needles; in general, of a self-inflicted beating to the body from which it takes, at best, weeks to recover." He concludes his analysis by dragging Jim Fixx through the mud again, as well as the "Unknown Soldier" of jogging who first pulled into Athens and promptly dropped dead after announcing the defeat of the Persians at Marathon.

Normally, this kind of snotty commentary would prompt a hot letter to the editor extolling the race as a challenge to the human spirit, but as the Queensboro Bridge finally opened into the last miles of the marathon, the cynical journalist sounded like Joshua to me. This was perhaps the first time I said to myself, "Maybe you should just stop. Maybe it would be okay to just stop." And again fate dropped a rose before me making that impossible.

As we started up the red carpeting that covered the grating on the bridge, a severely handicapped girl sat on a homemade wagon inching her way backward against gravity. She couldn't control her legs or arms very well but was able to push ahead with her feet. One of the Italians who had come over on the plane in a group stood jogging in place, watching her slow progress. His dark hair was slicked back like a swimmer's, his skin-tight leotards proclaimed bold calves, thighs, and buttocks in red, white, and green, like some Sicilian version of Superman. When it was clear the girl wasn't going to let him push her up the bridge, he bent over a face become monstrous with her effort, kissed her full on the mouth, and went on his way.

"Now that's Italian!"

Spectators were not allowed on the bridge, and for the first time in the race all the noise and hoopla from the crowds fell away. The silence was eerie as we ran high into the air approaching Manhattan. No automobiles, no foul exhaust fumes, as though war or some civic disaster had forced the population to desert the city. Giant girders pushed into the blue sky, iron struts twisted into a mammoth black honeycomb arching over distant waters. It was hard to believe the bridge was a manmade thing. In that deep silence my thoughts became almost physical objects. I was a slow-gliding hawk, my shadow playing over the World Trade Center, the Chrysler Building, the Empire State, high city of shiny metal beyond filth or poverty or fear.

Not long ago, at another race, mysteriously, a young athlete ran off the course and leaped over the handrail on such a bridge. The papers described it as one more tragic death brought on by the stress of competitive sports. But as I ran across the bridge I could almost imagine trying the thin air, like Icarus, climbing higher and higher in his ecstasy toward the brilliant sun.

The mind shuts down at such dangerous moments, a kind of psychological self-preservation. When there are no neurons left to translate the pain, a torture victim will mercifully pass out, and I suspect there must be some similar overload mechanism to handle mania. I was winging around in such euphoria that I grew faint. As we came off the bridge onto First Avenue thousands of New Yorkers smashed through the silence in greeting, like the blast of hot air an express train makes when it roars through the subway.

Marathon guides describe a sense of self you sometimes achieve in the race that is "elemental, childlike, and somehow connected to the essence of who you are." This stripped-down self made its way down from the blue heights and back into the exhausted runner on the bridge. The runner was a little stunned, unable to take it all in for the moment, and began to cry.

I realized I had better be a little careful or some well-meaning health-care worker might tackle me and force me onto a first aid cot. Coma and hyperthermia weren't the only symptoms of dehydration. I was a little terrified suddenly with the thought that maybe my emotional volatility *was* the result of some metabolic crisis I was going through. Like a melancholy Irishman lost in his "vin triste" who finally pulls himself together and closes up the bar, I ran to the next water station, drank a cup, and threw several more over my head and shoulders. My shirt and shorts were completely soaked and clung to me like cellophane. The sun was still bright, but a breeze had come up making the water uncomfortably cold. I looked like a shipwreck survivor as I fished out a couple of hard candies that had worked their way into my crotch and turned into sticky orange paste; or more, I thought, like an orangutan hanging around in his own muck on display for all the chic New Yorkers who dallied over brunch along First Avenue.

It was a straight shot up to Harlem now, four miles to the Willis Avenue Bridge for a token jog through the Bronx, then back through Harlem for the home stretch down Fifth Avenue and through Central Park. Looking uptown from the foot of First Avenue was as bleak an experience as looking into space on a night without moon or stars. I became conscious of my hip pain again and decided another Advil would be permissible. It was hours since the last dose when I started the race, well within the guidelines printed on the bottle. I also pulled into one of the portable johns that had appeared along the course. My urine didn't seem to be bloodstained anymore, so I was doubly relieved as I let the door bang behind me and started back into the race.

At the seventeen-mile marker I was able to put the hip pain in the background again and enjoy the "easy listening" station I had found on the radio.

There were far fewer people lining the streets now as we left the restaurant district in the 70's and 80's. This far north along First Avenue the excitement seemed to peter out, and people drifted into other Sunday amusements, doing the *New York Times* crossword puzzle, maybe taking a nap, or catching up on their laundry. Occasionally, a policeman standing alone beside a sawhorse barrier made a valiant effort to cheer on the runners, but with most of the crowd gone it sounded a little silly. Paper cups and trash filled the street. The wind was growing colder.

I was becoming a little bored myself, as a matter of fact. The race had become a rather lonely affair. When Tony Bennett came on the radio and began to sing of the loss of his heart in San Francisco, I was filled with a nostalgia that gave soul to the exquisite exhaustion I was feeling physically. My dad had told us

a thousand times how he had sailed out under the Golden Gate
Bridge on his way to World War II. Tony Bennett made that
memory live. In four years my dad would come back a tan, cocky
world traveler to sweep my mother off her feet and start his life.
But shipping out under the Golden Gate Bridge was to be the
loneliest moment in the entire life of a farm boy who had never
left the state of Pennsylvania before. For the thousandth time I
shared that loneliness as though I were another lost boy from
Pennsylvania on that ship who had no friends and felt he had
made the worst mistake of his life.

Funny how we still meet each other in music like this, my dad
and I, when there are important things about life that we can't
bring ourselves to say to each other. I know, for instance, that his
favorite Sinatra song is "When I Was Seventeen." That outra-
geously sentimental finale where old Blue Eyes thinks of the
autumn of his life and compares himself to aged wine still can
bring a tear to my eye when I think of my father. He's moody in
the fall, takes the season personally. I am as afraid of winter
then, as afraid of his death, as he is. But he will never say as
much, betrays his silence only in music, the way at Christmas-
time he sometimes goes off by himself for a day and we know
that in spite of his wife and children and grandchildren, he is still
grieving for his own dear mother who died and deserted him
fifty winters ago.

Can such melancholy be contagious, perhaps genetic? Over
the years I've come to see something desperate about the beauty
of fall. The last light, the last chance. Nature at odds with re-
demption, spirit at odds with instinct. The drama is played out
daily with trees set afire in burning golds and reds, while brown
bears relent finally, like exhausted children, and go to their dark
caves. Robert Penn Warren says that at this time he hears the
great geese hoot northward and does not know what is happening in his heart.

One of the few joys of aging, I imagine, is that you acquire a
personal sense of history, are able to look carefully at the various
people you have been over the years, compare them, possibly
learn something. How many different falls have I wondered

what was happening in my heart? Kicking through the horse chestnuts on my way to school. Taking first prize dressed as an orange crepe-paper pumpkin. Piles of burning leaves in all the neighbor yards turning the sky smoky blue after supper while we flitted around like little bats playing tag. Hunting field rats with my terrier as they fed on deserted stubble in the cornfields. "Mother, look at Lady, she's bleeding from behind," and Mother so remarkably unconcerned. Losing my brother to the monastery that same year, seeing how long I could hold myself in the form of a crucifix during prayer. The torture of trying not to touch myself and the certainty of God's condemnation when finally one day something seemed to break inside and fluid spurted out of me like the visible stain of sin. Watching the hair grow under my arms, the thin mustache. The mystery of my sisters' breasts. Spelling bees, scout camp, graduations. Seeing one day for the first time that my parents were growing old. Giving up on God after graduation and too many years of failure. The boy who seduced me on the plane to Switzerland, his student hotel, a wrestling match that passed for sex because we didn't know what else to do. Photo albums filled with holiday celebrations, vacations. Easter, Labor Day, Thanksgiving, Christmas, Easter, Labor Day, Thanksgiving, Christmas. The seasons parade through my life like film stars who are beginning to show wrinkles around the eyes and are more and more in need of good wardrobes and long shots to bring off the old glamour.

In a couple of years William and I will celebrate twenty of friendship, almost half of my life at that point. Unrelenting, this mathematical progression, but unrelenting too the way the years strengthen our feeling for each other like circles of growth on a great tree trunk. In how many oceans have we swum together, told how many jokes, driven how many miles. Once on a holiday in Casablanca we left the beach at three and stayed in bed until nearly midnight, when we came out for plates of shrimp and mayonnaise and cold white wine.

In a couple of years I'll begin the Indian summer of my life, and already my dear William has had his share of winter. I think of lightning rending the black sky in *King Lear,* proclaiming disorder in the universe, and the tragic injustices old age will heap on him. There was no storm as we lay in bed the night before William was to read his poem celebrating the Brooklyn Bridge centennial. But a fierce electrical storm raged through his poor brain, I suppose, as the blood vessel burst and ruined the elegant structures of his speech and thought. I was sure he was only joking as he flung his limbs about. I went to him then and found I could not pry his mouth open.

> Blow, winds, and crack your cheeks! rage! blow!
> You cataracts and hurricanoes, spout
> Till you have drenched our steeples, drowned the cocks!
> You sulph'rous and thought-executing fires,
> Vaunt-couriers of oak-cleaving thunderbolts,
> Singe my white head!

It's hard to imagine what he went through as I lay sleeping beside him that night. Of such a storm the Earl of Kent remarks to Lear, "Man's nature cannot carry / The affliction nor the fear."

At nineteen miles my muscle tissues cried out for oxygen the way children at play refuse to give up the thin last light of days that have already become diminished by the earth's sad distance from the sun. My tired bones seemed to translate the wilted city, the planet tilting and growing cold. I was coming to the legendary twenty-mile point in the marathon, in just one mile would confront the fabled Wall. This was what I had really trained for, preparing to face the unknown of my personal limits. The final miles of the race lay waiting for me like summer storm clouds building to a black head over the long heat of day.

I was amazed that runners of every age and both sexes still remained in the race, that it wasn't all just forty-year-old amateurs. We were a sickly lot by now, like refugees staggering across the border before the military junta sealed it forever. The field still remained a fair cross section of the runners that had started off together four hours ago on the Verrazano Bridge.

The little strip of Alexander Avenue that carried us into the Bronx was littered with broken glass, garbage, and other ghetto debris. The buildings were worn down with years of filth and disrepair. As I came over the Madison Avenue Bridge into Harlem, the northernmost point in the marathon course, someone had posted a hand-painted sign that read simply, "Say no to death." It didn't say otherwise the devil will get you, or advertise any particular Christian sect. A ghetto philosopher was simply painting the big picture as we came running into his slum pushing ourselves to the max. I thought of the old guy in a wheelchair at the outset of the race who had had only enough energy to wave his hand a little at the wrist like the pendulum of a clock as the runners passed him by. He wasn't strong enough to clap his hands, but there he was just the same, sitting in the sunshine, part of it all, cheering the runners on to the finish line. Say no to death. It was more moving than I could have believed. And harder to subscribe to than I would have believed, as well.

In one of William's best poems, "a commotion of years washes over" the adventurer Trelawny, and he recalls the drowning death of his young friend the poet Shelley. "Though I am still a strong swimmer / I can feel this channel widen as I swim," he says in his dream. At this point in the race I also felt trapped in such a disturbing bad dream.

It seemed like hours since I had seen the last marker announcing nineteen miles and the prospect of meeting the Wall. Could I be banging my head against the Wall even now? Time and space had become hallucinatory, a kind of Einsteinian meltdown. The coordinates fixing reality were subsumed into an overriding fifth dimension of nightmare.

Spectators filled the streets again as we ran deeper into Harlem, lots of people carrying on as if it were Carnival. Groups of women stood outside the storefront churches in feathered hats and purple sequins, clapping in unison under a sign that proclaimed in neon lights that "God is Love." Other ladies took it all in with greater aplomb, watching from within a cloud of marijuana that wafted over to us like incense as we ran by. Ahead of me I noticed a little black girl about ten years old hiding something in her hand, sizing up each runner that came by with great white eyes. She was shy as a squirrel and wasn't going to have any luck giving away the piece of candy or orange or whatever she was offering by hanging back so carefully. As I came up to her I slowed down to see what secret she was hiding. A tiny toy koala bear, brown and furry, peeked up over her small fist. She didn't say a word, but it was clear I was being introduced.

"Pretty late in the day to still be running a marathon, wouldn't you agree, Mr. Bear?" I thought. "Would you like to wrap your huggie arms around my little finger and help me finish this goddamn race?"

In an instant I had taken the koala from her hand and was running ahead again. Suddenly I had the awful feeling that maybe she *wasn't* bestowing this toy on some special runner she was waiting to find, that maybe I had just mugged a schoolgirl for her little mascot. But when I turned back to find her in the crowd she gave me a shy smile and waved to me as though I were her secret lover. I clipped Mr. Bear to my shirt and blew her a big kiss that lit up her face.

I wouldn't have parted with that toy bear for anything in the world, but that kiss almost did me in. For almost five hours I had been pushing straight ahead, step after step, in single-minded forward motion toward the finish line. Twisting my body at the waist to look back at her sent a wrenching pain through my groin muscles that was like being processed in a meat grinder. I swallowed the last Advil I had rationed for the race and rumbled on a hundred yards or so like a car that has suddenly blown a tire and is struggling to keep from running off the road. It was difficult to get back into the rhythm that had become as mindless as breathing. After a while the pain was beginning to wear off a little, the way the sting eventually fades out of a burn, when a second miracle nearly undid me. My heart started flopping around like a seabird in an oil slick when I looked up to see the twenty-one-mile marker just ahead.

Oh Jesus, oh Jesus. Some sweet genius had simply deleted the infamous twenty-mile marker from the course to help us over the psychological hurdle of the Wall—out of sight, out of mind. I had already broken through, it seemed, was already beginning mile twenty-two of the race.

My spirit began to ricochet off the walls and leap up into the trees, but all I could bring myself to do physically by way of celebration was give a single high-pitched burst of a laugh. The guy in front of me winced like a monk startled in the midst of prayer. At this point in the race runners were saving their energy, and you rarely heard a peep from anyone. Last year two hundred people were treated at the twenty-mile medical tent in spite of all the balloons and hundreds of green megaphones given out to boisterous children. The cots were filled with runners with a range of ailments from muscle spasm to collapse. Beyond mile twenty the body had spent its reserves and was running on something other than blood and oxygen. All the guidebooks will tell you that the body has nothing left to give now, and the only thing that enables you to keep it from falling into a heap is will power. Physical stamina has nothing to do with the race at this point. And this is precisely the challenge that veterans of the marathon have entered the race again for, to see what their bodies and souls will make of it all this year, to see if they can't reverse time by doing even better than they did last year.

For me, no particularly gargantuan act of will was fueling my body's effort. I didn't need to consciously prod myself along. The little engine driving my soul kicked into overdrive and produced something like dream power. It simply happened while I looked on, like levitation. You try for hours, work yourself into a splitting headache, and when you finally give up, sure enough the knife slowly rises from the table, or you notice that your feet are floating six inches off the floor.

At one level, of course, every yard was very real agony and hard won. Pain emanated from any number of sources, and my exhausted body was begging me to pull off the road and sit under a tree for a while. But at another level the race was proving to me in a way that was unique in my experience how more than physical we are, how clearly other we can be than the particular shell we happen to be inhabiting, the "husk," as William would say, or the little house we "abandon" when we die.

I was certainly in my body, but not necessarily *of* it, I guess, like that contemporary cartoon of a movie that illustrates so nicely the Cartesian dualism of mind over matter. In the postnuclear world of *Beyond Thunderdome* society is run by a nasty little midget named Masterblaster who rides around on the shoulders of an idiot giant and makes him do his bidding. This rather successful partnership has kept the world in slavery, producing energy out of pig manure, until it meets up with Mel Gibson and Tina Turner, queen of the Thunderdome gladiators—can any tyrant, regardless of IQ, really have all his marbles if he messes with Tina Turner? The body's travails are interesting. There may be a certain curiosity about how precisely we fall apart trying to run 26.2 miles. But in the end who wants to hear the gory details down to the last blister?

The doctor puts on his concerned face with his white jacket to listen to the tired aches and pains of humanity once again. Who *isn't* arthritic, or nursing an ulcer, or having a tough time taking care of an invalid at home? Everybody has something. It's why we all understand the blues. Don't we have a moral obligation to tell an off-color joke every now and then? Why belabor the "affliction, the fear"? Why would I want to hear the trouble you went through having your baby, for example, when I've got the sweet little rug rat in my arms?

The next four miles would be as tough as anything I would ever do in my life, but I decided to keep myself tuned in to that part of me sitting on my shoulder, like Masterblaster overseeing the production of methane in the bowels of the city. I tried to take in the scenery, the way I did those Sundays Dad would pile us all into the car and we'd drive into the country to visit our favorite dairy for ice cream. Just out for the ride.

One of the sweet things I noticed was the sympathetic look in the eyes of spectators who chose to stand along the final few miles of our trial. The compassion in those eyes was mysterious, beautiful. God's own sweet grace seemed to play across their faces like light dappling a forest.

Another puzzle preoccupied me as we left Fifth Avenue and entered Central Park. Twenty youngsters sat deserted in their wheelchairs like cabbages that someone had forgotten to protect against an unexpected frost. These "floppy" babies had grown into "floppy" children. Their heads undulated on little stems, their limbs waved slowly like seaweed on the ocean floor. Nurses had parked them along the curb several hours ago, perhaps, and they could only wait in the cold until someone decided to wipe their noses or take them back in again. One little boy with thick black eyebrows and lashes looked at me as he pushed himself up in his chair. His skin was unblemished ivory, as though he hadn't grown past his smooth baby skin. By working hard and turning his arms like a windmill he was finally able to right himself. He gave me a big drooly smile, as though he had just won the New York middleweight wrestling championship.

"All right," I shouted to him. "Way to go."

I pretended to miss a step and fall into a stumble. I screwed up my face and began flapping my arms around, mirroring *his* effort as though I had cerebral palsy too, or was a fledgling that had fallen out of the nest. I was mocking him, all right. Goofing around, yes, but I was teasing him in a way I wouldn't have tried unless I happened to be his older brother or unless a marathon had worn down my self-consciousness. But he was a big boy, didn't take it amiss. He started to laugh and laugh, and so did the girl sitting beside him, like two sweet little geese honking at the moon.

Now as I came deeper into the heart of Central Park there were exhausted runners lining the road who had already finished the race. They limped along slowly clutching the silver thermal capes about them and eating a Milky Way or an apple or a bagel. Garbage containers were filled with green Perrier bottles that had been shoved into their hands at the finish line, enough rosebud vases to supply every café table in Manhattan.

"Hang in there," the newly triumphant called out to those of us still marking time in limbo. "It's not far now." Runners gave exhausted grunts that seemed to respond, "Easy for you to say." There were plenty of fans in the crowd who realized that, if anything, the latecomers needed a cheering section more than those who had finished the race hours ago. Even though the stadium seemed to be emptying, the fans were going to stay until the last batter was retired, the last inning played out.

"Just a mile and a half," some guy shouted to each runner who traipsed by him. He waved them on like a frantic traffic cop in rush hour. "Move it, lady. Move it. Move it. Move it." I forced a smile just like everyone else that came poking by. Except for pit stops, I had been running nonstop for exactly five hours.

As we turned the corner onto Central Park South the guy running beside me looked over and smiled. Number 13287. A nice smile and bright eyes. He wore a singlet, shorts, and headband all stamped with the New York Marathon logo: a stick man running on a big red apple. His mustache and goatee were flecked salt and pepper, and his glasses were the wire-rimmed FDR type. But I could tell he was about my own age.

He had an odd running gait, something between walking and jogging, but his muscle tone was great and he looked remarkably fresh to be coming into the home stretch of a marathon. We were running at the same pace, side by side, and though we couldn't see it, we could almost feel the finish line pulling us into the running chutes that were lined by picket fences to restrain family and friends. We were bringing it on home, like the final thrust of lovemaking just before you let yourself go and lose consciousness a while of who you are.

I could tell my sidekick wanted to talk to me, wanted to share a sense of pride and relief and valediction. Maybe he was running alone like me, maybe he didn't have anyone waiting for him at the finish line either. William would be waiting for me at Paul's apartment instead, since there was no telling how long it would take me to finish, or *if* I would finish.

Even when I get off an airplane and no one is scheduled to meet me, I still find myself looking around expectantly. Everyone else is hugging his wife while the kids cluster about yapping for a present. Everywhere there are little bursts of reunion, a child running to Grandma, someone shedding tears, while you stand around like the ghost of Christmas past. Having someone meet you almost seems to be part of the landing procedure, and if you pick up your luggage in silence by yourself, somehow you haven't really arrived.

We ran facing straight ahead, oblivious to the spectators cheering us on, hopeful for any sign of a finish line.

"How you doing?" my running mate asked, and gave me the same shy smile.

"Okay," I said. "How about you?"

"I'm doing great," he said. "It's been a beautiful run."

I had let my form slip a little now and bowed my head as I ran. I thought of the past hours, feeling the weight of the day settle on my soul. How many miles had I run to prepare for this moment? How many mornings did I pull myself out of bed and start by lacing up my jogging shoes?

The pace and vigor of my strides had diminished, but I knew I would make it to the finish line in respectable form, all I ever really hoped for during the months of preparation. One of those terribly hot summer days when I was training, a song came on the headset that was a simple idiot refrain set to atomic bomb rock and roll. As I came to Ryan's Hill I set the volume on maximum until my ears nearly bled, making a conscious decision to let the stupid lyrics function as a prayer. For all their banality they suited some personal song of gratitude that was welling up in me. Louder, brighter, stronger, I danced to the very crest.

As I began the final mile of the New York City Marathon, however, I was not dancing, I was not singing. Now it was a little hard to concentrate on anything other than running, as though I had gone blind. The contrasts wanted to run together, as the dark-haired lady says in William's poem, and I was left with only peripheral vision. My body seemed to lack the energy required to run and talk and take in the pageant igniting up ahead all at the same time. But I knew in a short while I would be able to feel the joy of it fully and was amazed by the fact.

"You know, I'm dying," I said, "but it really wasn't as bad as I thought. I mean, it could have been a lot worse."

We were like two tenderfoot Boy Scouts just gassing about Life in a dark pup tent hours after the camp leader had declared lights out.

"Want to run back to the Verrazano Bridge?"

"Right."

My running partner turned out to be a teacher at City College, three kids, fourth marathon. We chatted wearily. His wife's interest in his running had paled, but she would have a good supper ready for him when he got home. I bragged about William a little, the usual, decided for no particular reason to keep my love for him to myself. "Lights out, you guys. Knock it off and go to sleep, or there'll be no boating tomorrow."

And miraculously enough, an enormous red, white, and blue banner announcing the finish line eventually appeared around a bend. A giant clock floated over the banner like the crown of heaven. I felt as though I were running toward the clock in slow motion—could "feel this channel widen as I swim." I was as confused as any longhorn in a roundup trying to figure out which running chute to feed myself into without getting trampled. There was such a great crush of runners and timekeepers and volunteers and onlookers I didn't quite understand what was happening.

In what must surely be the most exquisite anticlimax of my life, I somehow managed to pass under the banner in the middle of my partner's farewell. "Been nice running with you." He smiled and waved goodbye. Only when a pretty girl placed a silver medal with a blue and white ribbon around my neck did I realize that I had actually run the New York City Marathon.

Tomorrow's *New York Post* would rank my new friend just ahead of me even though we both passed through the chutes at exactly five hours fifteen minutes and five seconds. They could have ranked me last for all I cared. I had run the entire New York City Marathon and crossed the finish line standing up. I couldn't get over what a wonderful thing had just happened.

The dust of the long day's run washed from my eyes. I was

able to focus on things, "to see the extraordinary data" once again as the crowd thinned out and I slowed down to a limp.

People began to look after us now, and no one raised any objection to the care they offered. The simple act of walking again was a shock. Every abused muscle and ligament took its little revenge for the nasty trip it had been forced to endure. A television commercial for Anacin would have a million scarlet arrows pointing to every joint and bone in my body.

One volunteer fastened a silver cape around my neck, and another smacked a big red apple into the palm of my hand. Congratulations from the City of New York. I bit in with a chomp, and it was just as sweet as having dessert with Eve in the Garden of Paradise. The taste was almost visible.

Runners walked along grunting with pain, sucking in air, massaging their muscles. Some immediately took off their shoes to check blisters or some other little emergency. Some runners just sprawled under a tree despite encouragement from the officials to keep walking. The finish-line area looked a little like the scene of an airplane crash, bodies and debris strewn about, solicitous helpers ministering where they could.

I was freezing cold now, soaking wet in the chill late afternoon, without a carbohydrate left to stoke up the fires again. I found the bus where I had stored my gym bag and thanked God for the genius of organization who had arranged to have our buses meet us so we would have dry clothing to change into at the end of the race.

Men and women made halfhearted attempts to hide their nakedness as they slipped out of their running shorts and into warm-up outfits. But having sex at this point would have been as likely as it would if we'd been a bunch of eunuchs just back from a full day's shopping at Bloomingdale's with the harem.

Boyfriends met girlfriends now and vice versa. Husbands met wives. There was a lot of hugging, crying, and patting on the back. Some folks just got dressed in silence and kept their own counsel as they left the park. Finishing the race wasn't something you could talk about right away; there was an emotional emptiness, a psychological letdown that somehow corresponded to the depleted metabolism of the body, and it would take a little time for the reservoir to fill up again. I wanted to hang around a while and soak up the good vibrations emanating from all the triumphant wrecks staggering around the finish area. But their achievement was very private too, and I felt a little lost or out of place. Besides, I was a wreck myself. I couldn't imagine finding Grace and Rudy in that mob and hoped they would understand my decision to get home as soon as I could, where dear Willie would be waiting for me. I would call Grace from Paul's apartment later to see how she finished and let her know I made it.

When I finally got into fresh socks and long pants, a snug running jacket, and a clean, dry cap I felt a heck of a lot better. It was like washing away the blood and wrapping up the wound with a sterile dressing—the damage wasn't diminished any, but I *felt* a whole lot better about it. Only "tincture of time" would really do much for me at this point.

As I limped out of the park I indulged myself in a hot dog with all the fixings. I thought maybe the hot dog guy might congratulate me or something, but he'd been pushing those dogs all day long and now the party was over. He gave me back my change without a word.

I got exactly two blocks before I went into the bushes to throw up pieces of hot dog, apple, onions with mustard, and a soup of half-digested Milky Way. I'd have to rest a while before I could keep anything down. Later tonight we could all go out to celebrate. I just longed to soak in a tub full of scalding water. I started walking again and stopped in a chichi pharmacy, where, to my amazement, the clerk fished a carton of Epsom salts from behind the counter. Even blue-haired ladies on the Upper East Side needed a hot bath with Epsom salts from time to time.

One fear I had when I planned getting home from the race was that taxis would be impossible to find and that I wouldn't be in good enough shape to walk the mile back to Paul's apartment from the finish line. But even though I moved like an arthritic praying mantis, I was able to make my way up to 71st Street slowly without too much difficulty. I got into the ancient eleva-

tor in Paul's building, let the accordion door bang closed behind
me, and started the slow ascent to the fourth floor.

William's brown corduroy trousers came into view as I rose to
the window on the elevator door at the fourth floor. The dear old
friends who had agreed to spend the afternoon with him while I
ran the marathon had apparently seen me coming on the street
and sent William out to meet me. I stepped out of the elevator,
and there he was, the old sweetie, beaming with joy for me,
crying a little, saying "good, good," over and over.

I was home. William's joy ignited my own, the way it does
with friendship. And despite our friends waiting to greet me, I
took William in my arms and just stood in the hallway holding
on the way I'd done so often in my life, except this time he was
supporting me. I was a fighter pilot coming in for a landing, a
little busted, maybe, but I'd put that baby safely down on deck.
Next time it might be William's turn. The sea might get a little
choppy, the ship might be hard to find in a night without stars. I
remember once I brought him to the emergency room on a very
close call. The doctors pumped his chest and tried every drug
they could think of for two full hours before they were able to
start his engine up again. I hovered over him and dreamed up a
layman's version of extreme unction. We all have to play chaplain for one another from time to time.

It would be foolish of me to think that William won't come to
the end of his marathon someday. "Men must endure / Their
going hence, even as their coming hither; / Ripeness is all,"
Edgar says to his tired old father in *King Lear*. I know there will
be more illnesses, and plenty of other challenges, as we run our
race.

Being a caregiver may keep me from presiding over General
Motors, or climbing Mount Kilimanjaro, but it's a valid calling
just the same. I may not have children or hold office in the
United States Senate. My life may seem limited in scope to
some people, even selfish, perhaps. But William and I help each
other like "bandaged comrades" so we don't stumble in the
dark. I'm proud to share and support his life.

I think of the sweet letter Josephine sent to us recently, how William's light still burns brightly for others in spite of his stroke:

I can't resist this note to say how, *how* much your poetry has meant, and means, to me. In this past unlovable year, it has been a sustenance and a model, has both heartened and humbled me.

I wish you and Richard weren't going to be so far from us in the next weeks—but spring *will* come; in fact, I cheered myself on this gray day with the inconspicuous fact that the sun rose a tiny bit earlier and set tonight a tiny bit later. With our love to you both.

Josephine

It's a little like beating Death at his own game when you can outmaneuver all the tragedy life wants to set in your way. We won't give up the world's dear light easily, or apologize for the pleasure we take in it.

Last winter good old Bill Barrett wrote an exercise for William's speech therapy, which I found on the coffee table after he'd gone home. Barrett ended the lesson by quoting Eliot, who was quoting Spenser, I think. The point was to remind William of our own bright river in New London to which we would soon return. The refrain is a bit somber, the rhyme a little trite, but sometimes when I'm bored with running I sing the lines to myself as I jog along the riverbank:

> Sweet Thames, run softly till I end my song,
> Sweet Thames, run softly for I speak not loud or long.

I pulled out of my bear hug with William, disengaged from my reverie, and fended off the old friends who stood waiting to congratulate me.

"I'll tell you all about the race later, Anthony," I said. "Right now I'm dying to sink into a hot tub and just let my body parts float to the surface. Do you mind?"

"Of course not," he said.

"I'll come out when I've shriveled into a raisin, and we can go to La Goulule for oysters and filet mignon. No pasta tonight. What do you say, Willie?"

"Sure."

And we all went in.

E P I L O G U E

As I finished writing this account William won the 1988 Pulitzer Prize in poetry for *Partial Accounts*. He is speaking better all the time, and he has just edited a selection of his prose pieces for publication.

I'm still running and hope to try the marathon again one day. *Et la fête continue.*

December 22, 1988
Bethesda, Maryland